WINNIPEG

D0438856

WITHDRAWN

MEET PARIS OYSTER

MEET PARIS OYSTER

A LOVE AFFAIR
WITH THE PERFECT FOOD

. . .

MIREILLE GUILIANO

GRAND CENTRAL
Life & Style
NEW YORK • BOSTON

Copyright © 2014 by Mireille Guiliano

All rights reserved. In accordance with the U.S. Copyright Act of 1976, the scanning, uploading, and electronic sharing of any part of this book without the permission of the publisher constitute unlawful piracy and theft of the author's intellectual property. If you would like to use material from the book (other than for review purposes), prior written permission must be obtained by contacting the publisher at permissions@hbgusa.com. Thank you for your support of the author's rights.

Grand Central Life & Style
Hachette Book Group
1290 Avenue of the Americas
New York, NY 10019

www.GrandCentralLifeandStyle.com

Printed in the United States of America

RRD-C

First Edition: November 2014
10 9 8 7 6 5 4 3 2 1

Grand Central Life & Style is an imprint of Grand Central Publishing. The Grand Central Life & Style name and logo are trademarks of Hachette Book Group, Inc.

The Hachette Speakers Bureau provides a wide range of authors for speaking events. To find out more, go to www.HachetteSpeakersBureau.com or call (866) 376-6591.

The publisher is not responsible for websites (or their content) that are not owned by the publisher.

Library of Congress Cataloging-in-Publication Data

Guiliano, Mireille, 1946-
    Meet Paris oyster : a love affair with the perfect food / Mireille Guiliano.
        pages cm
    Includes index.
    ISBN 978-1-4555-2408-2 (hardback)—ISBN 978-1-4555-2409-9 (ebook)—ISBN 978-1-4789-8302-6 (audio download)   1. Cooking (Oysters)   2. Raw foods.   3. Food habits—France—Paris.   I. Title.
    TX754.O98G85 2014
    641.6'94—dc23

2014002848

Contents

MEET PARIS
OYSTER

OUVERTURE

You might not be able to see the world through an oyster shell, but if you press your nose up to the window of a tiny oyster shack of a restaurant in Paris's Saint Germain-des-Prés area and view the dozen or so people feasting on platters of oysters and sipping wine, you *can* see Paris—the people, the passions, the culture, the Frenchness, the appetites (gastronomic and other-wise), the seductions, the fashion, the locals and the tourists, the banter, the drama—and feel the pulse of the city and its people. Welcome to Paris Oyster.

The place of the shelled bivalve in French culture and life underlines the difference between France and the rest of the world, and between Paris and other world capitals.

Where else on New Year's Eve do you see crates of oysters

being proffered one after another on the sidewalks and in the food stores? What other city has 250 restaurants serving oysters and 25 devoted to not much else? Where else do you find people excited to rapture over slurping slippery, gross-looking chunks of flesh down their gullets? Ummm... *délicieux*.

Oysters grow all over the world, and people the world over eat them. They have never been so broadly and readily available and diverse. It can be argued that they have never been so popular. Yet oysters in Paris are part of the French culture and identity... and the French are very patriotic in their types and accompaniments.

It is a pleasure to introduce you to a lovely enclave of Paris and share advice on how to open, eat, and learn to love oysters, perhaps enticing those of you who have not yet tried a raw oyster to take the leap and give this most nutritious of foods a try. I will also share some implicit and explicit cultural commentary and some of my thoughts regarding what France's love affair with the oyster says about my native land. Taken together, braided, I hope these various elements come together into a work that indeed shows the world through an oyster shell in Paris.

This partial slice-of-life play, this *comédie humaine*, is about pleasure and celebrating life, about *joie de vivre* and *art de vivre*. Perhaps enjoy it with a glass of Champagne or Sancerre.

1

Huîtrerie Régis, Paris

The initial tip came nearly a decade ago from my Parisian friend Mélanie, who loves oysters almost as much as I do. "Huîtrerie Régis has just opened in your neighborhood," she e-mailed. "You must go; it's on the short street between the Marché Saint-Germain and the Boulevard Saint-Germain and like no other place in the world...Sorry, but they don't take reservations." She knew I would love it.

So I went. And went. Between October and May, whenever I am in Paris, it is my *cantine*, though it is hard to call one of the tiniest restaurants possible a cafeteria. The oyster has a lot to do with why I go to this seemingly one-dish restaurant, but really it is much more than that: a *huîtrerie* is basically an oyster bar, and there are plenty in town, but this is one of a kind. For one thing, as a regular pointed out to me early on and only semi-jokingly: "Régis picks his customers. And the customer is not zee king here, Régis is." It is a restaurant with personality and attitude and the highest quality.

I almost blew it with Régis on my first visit. When on a lovely fall day my early-morning plane arrival from New York became a late-morning arrival, I was starving and a bit frustrated, so I thought a few oysters would reconcile me with the world. Plus, I was eager to test this new place. I arrived at almost 2 p.m., but I wasn't sure they'd serve me as the place was pretty packed (it doesn't take much for it to be filled), with only one gentleman seemingly ready to leave. A minute later, I had a table. I felt lucky. A great little table *pour moi*.

The menu arrived immediately, and a fetchingly pert young waitress took my order two minutes later. And then I waited, and waited, and waited. In a one-dish restaurant there is no amuse or appetizers or even a bread basket before the food, and the key in my head had still not switched from New York to Paris *art de vivre*. My stomach was growling, and I was wondering why it was taking so long to shuck a dozen oysters. Meanwhile, most customers were almost done or chatting over their espresso. I sat, feeling hungrier and hungrier. Edward, my husband of many decades, knows well that I can get grumpy fast when I'm very hungry. I was almost ready to ask if they had forgotten me. Plus, I had been in such a rush to get to the restaurant while it was still serving (2 p.m. is a common cut-off time) that I came without my smart phone or anything to read. So I just sat there, and my expression surely turned into a glare. Régis no doubt read my face and did whatever it took to "lengthen the pleasure," or test me, as I later learned. He simply ignored me.

Fortunately for me, I overheard a regular next to me mentioning how Régis was in a bad mood today after a morning telephone argument with the credit card machine sales rep, and so patience was required (or was the man observing the show and trying to give me a heads-up?). That was definitely a hint I took as a favor and kept quiet . . . and waited, and waited, and contemplated the restaurant. Apparently, as I learned after a few visits and conversations with regulars, for someone like Régis, who gets up very early six days a week, rushing is not in order, and those who are in a hurry better go elsewhere. Wow, how is that for customer service? That's how I learned his number one rule: "Nobody gives me pressure." A few months later, a single man at the table next to me described what Régis calls difficult customers, or in his lexicon *bêtes noires*, and his way of turning them down: Let them wait . . . and wait. It's his definition of the ultimate luxury in business! Customers should be willing to wait.

And so, my platter of oysters was delivered twenty-eight

minutes after the order was taken. I was hot inside but tried to be zen or at least look zen. But then it seems that the love affair had started. Without my being aware of it, he discreetly looked at how I approached the bivalves: how I smelled them, tasted them (I had a hard time not devouring them, but then one does not do this with oysters), and followed with a piece of bread with a thick layer of salted butter. I felt right in some sort of gastronomic heaven, and it surely did wonders for the look on my face. *Et voilà.* Now I somehow had gained approved blessing, though nothing is ever acquired quickly in the world of Régis. And I certainly was not yet a member of the club.

The "short street" is rue Montfaucon in the sixth arrondissement. Huîtrerie Régis is at number 3. Now imagine a storefront space that's about 18 feet wide and 15 feet deep. That's it, the entire restaurant. Enter the windowed exterior and off to the right, say about six inches, is a small stand-up bar, more of a serving counter, behind which stands the shucker, the waitress, often Régis, the oysters, the wine, the coffee machine, the sink the size of a pasta pot, the silverware, the glassware, everything. The back wall is the "wine cellar." A little room is squared off in the opposite back corner, the smallest toilette/WC possible. On one side a table and chairs abut the closet.

In the "dining room," there are seven small tables accommodating fourteen people. *Snug* is the operative word. The majority of the tables have inches at most of separation between them. But it works, partly because the French have a way of isolating, encircling themselves in privacy in public. The way Americans are well known for talking to strangers right and left in restaurants, the French are not. The raised platters of oysters also help as territorial delineators. Outside are a couple of sidewalk tables for "smokers" or for those waiting for a table inside or a take-out order of shucked oysters.

Yet this is a spotless, soulful gem of a fancy oyster shack in white and blue, some gold feathers hanging from the ceiling (a holiday fixture), and an interesting large paintingesque work of art on the back wall. Some of us, in a mode of seaside/cityscape fantasy, have decided that when we sit against the back wall facing the outside, we have a seat with a *vue sur la mer* (sea view). When is a street vista not a sea? You may think the attractive decor is the work of a woman, but it's all Régis and his sensibilities and sense of aesthetics. What makes the place a tad fancy and indicates that the owner takes the oysters seriously are the white tablecloths with real napkins, real silverware, and beautiful simple plates in white-and-blue porcelain (designed by a Brazilian female artist friend of Régis), and real service (a trio—where the man who shucks is part of the action, the young waitress is superattentive to your needs, and then there is Régis, *un personnage attachant*, a combination of charm, humor, and the ability to engage that Frenchwomen love. And he is…and complicated and comical and demanding and moody). And then there are the oysters…zee best. So, it works. It all works.

Consider the menu: it's simple. On one sheet there are three tasting formulas: (1) twelve oysters *fines de claires*, a glass of muscadet, and coffee; (2) two types of oysters, six of each with a glass of Sancerre and coffee; and (3) two types of oysters, six of each and six large shrimp. Then there is the second sheet, with Marennes oysters, all by the dozen, going from *fines de claires* to *spéciales de claires* and the rare and most expensive *pousses en claires*; the Belons (second most expensive and not often available); the *praires* (clams); and when available and up to Régis's standard, *oursins* (sea urchins). Again, the quality of the oysters and beyond is very high here, with the least expensive formula costing 25 euros. Not cheap. And at the bottom of that page are some items for non–oyster lovers perhaps dragged here by oyster lovers: terrine of scallops; huge Madagascar shrimp by the dozen; *assiette de saucisson* (a plate of perhaps a dozen slices of dry sausage); the cheese of the day; and the one and only dessert, *tarte aux pommes*, made by the master himself every morning.

The wine list is one page, too: a Roederer Champagne (noblesse oblige); one muscadet; two Pouilly-Fumé; seven Sancerre white and seven red; a few Burgundies and Bordeaux, some Charentes wines; and a list of digestifs, particularly Armagnac. The coffee is Lavazza. *C'est tout.* That's all.

Sunday Lunch at Huîtrerie Régis

In terms of weather, it is a common late-fall Parisian day: partly cloudy with a temperature of 43 degrees Fahrenheit. Walking down the short street toward the restaurant, we see a couple dressed for winter sitting at one of the two tiny outdoor sidewalk tables in front of the restaurant. They are not eating. They have not eaten. They are talking to an animated Régis, who is standing by the table in shirtsleeves.

Edward and I enter relatively late for lunch, with the time approaching 2 p.m., but it is a Sunday, after all. A distinguished-looking couple is standing and ready to leave. He is wearing a tie and jacket with a Legion of Honor pin on his lapel. She wears a black coat with a mink collar. Neighborhood folks. There are always some at Régis. It is also hard to remember a time at the restaurant when one of its fourteen seats was not occupied by someone Japanese. It seems the Japanese love oysters and *fruits de mer*, and Régis is known in Japan based upon some reports that his are the finest oysters in Paris. True. A Japanese couple are seated and reverently eating their oysters. There is a youngish French couple, a mixed couple—the man is French, the woman is not—and some out-of-towners, Brits by the sound of their voices.

There are Belons today, so we order six each and six *fines de claires spéciales* no. 3. And four shrimp, the big delicious

Madagascar type. The bread from Kayser bakery comes, the butter and sauce mignonette come, Régis comes. Régis is medium height for a Frenchman, which means not tall. He's a tad stocky in build but firm, with brown hair, bushy eyebrows in *accent circonflexe* (reverse V) shape, and a salt-and-pepper mustache. When he smiles some attractive dimples emerge, though when he is not so happy his forehead wrinkles into sinuous heavy furrows. He likes to speak in a hushed voice with his customers, a trait of respect for the others around him, though when a bunch of pals show up he tends to be more demonstrative and loud.

"What do you want to drink?" he asks us. We debate Champagne or Sancerre. We engage him in a discussion of Sancerre, his favorite accompaniment, and he is keen on his two producers, Daniel Crochet and Alphonse Mellot, each of whom produces several different bottlings from difficult crus. We choose the biodynamic Plante des Prés 2011 Crochet— a lovely, elegant Sancerre, drier than most but with centered fruit.

A tall, casually dressed man with what looks like a three-day-old beard walks in (anyone who walks into this tiny restaurant commands center stage) and says loudly: "Do you serve Arabs here?" Régis replies firmly, "No." "Do you serve Arabs here?" "No," and this time Régis swings his arm in emphasis. "Do you serve Arabs here?" "No," even more loudly, and Régis and the guy burst out laughing. The man is obviously Arab. They go outside and talk with another man standing there.

In France there is a lot of banter and teasing, especially when men get together (not to say women don't play the game—my mother was great at it—but for men it is part of their cultural baptism). Régis loves and excels at this. Being witty is something of a national sport, and the things people say while playing are sometimes shocking to those from another culture. But it is all part of the game, which was raised to a national virtue in the seventeenth-century court of Louis XIV when epigrammatic cleverness and the mode of being witty were much admired. To wit, the wits.

Back at the *huîtrerie*, the original couple are still sitting there, just outside our table's window, not eating. It is after three, and we are up to the fabulous apple tart and down to our last (okay, it's Sunday lunch!) sip of wine.

Régis is nowhere to be found; he has gone off somewhere. The tall "Arab" returns and chats with Alain, the first-rate *écailler* (shucker), and pours himself a glass of a red wine from the Loire, a Saumur. We couldn't see, but perhaps Alain passed him an oyster or two. He departs, consuming all in perhaps three minutes.

The restaurant is winding down. People keep coming in, asking if they are still serving, and, hearing "*Non,*" take a card then walk away.

Régis returns carrying about eight loaves or so of brown bread. Kayser is a long-established, well-respected baker in Paris with a number of outlets (and now franchising globally). "On Sunday the Kayser bakery is closed, so I have to go to a bakery that's not close," he says in passing and begins preparation for the evening service.

We order two cafés. We overhear Régis and the waitress—they are about six feet away; everything in the restaurant is about six feet away—discussing the merits of GPS versus printed road maps. The girl, who is in her early twenties and speaks enough English to handle the room, as Régis and Alain do not speak any English, is, curiously, a fan of the printed maps. Régis prefers GPS.

It is 3:30. We close the restaurant.

2

WHY EAT OYSTERS?

There are several compelling reasons to eat oysters. How about because they give us pleasure? That's one reason. Why eat oysters? Because they are nutritional powerhouses that are good for us. Oysters are not only delicious, they're also one of the most nutritionally well-balanced of foods, containing protein, carbohydrates, and lipids.

It's strange that oysters are not recommended more often as being good for one's health, as they are rich sources of antioxidants and omega-3 fatty acids, which have been the high-impact nutrition darlings of the press and physicians for a while. So, eating oysters twice a week is part of a good cardiac diet.

Oysters are filled with vitamins and minerals and specifically an excellent source of vitamins A, B_1, B_2, B_{12}, C, and D. Four to five oysters provide the daily recommended amounts of iron, copper, iodine, magnesium, calcium, zinc, manganese, selenium, and phosphorus. How is that for charging your immune system and maintaining good health? The iron helps against anemia; the phosphorus and minerals are good for your teeth and bones; the B vitamins are useful for red cell formation, blood coagulation, and energy; and I could go on. *And* four or five oysters add up to far fewer calories than a glass of milk—more like that of a fresh peach. I am not sure why, but oysters are generally ordered in multiples of three, as in a half dozen, a dozen, or perhaps just three of one kind (or three of this kind and three of that kind). At ten to fifteen calories per oyster, you can do the math. Minimal calories and maximum nutritional value. Naturally, the type, size, and origin of an oyster add some variation to the values, but overall, the benefits and values are sound. And, surprising to me, oysters are not high in sodium, even though they are raised in salt water and taste salty, but that salty taste comes mostly from the seawater liquid one consumes from the shell with the oyster's fleshy body. You'd have to eat and drink a lot of oysters to raise your blood pressure.

Before I go on with nutrition, let me interject one important observation about oysters and pleasure. Do you know what pairs exceedingly well with oysters? Friends. So, combined with being an excellent meal in themselves, oysters are an exceptional anti-aging food—one of the foods that you can eat more and not less of as you age.

For a long time, oysters were thought to contain high amounts of (bad) cholesterol, but now that the distinction has been made between bad cholesterol and good cholesterol, and new methods of calculating cholesterol levels are more accurate, oysters no longer make the watch list. Just the opposite. Chromatography has enabled us to identify the different kinds of sterols found in shellfish. What was thought of as cholesterol turned out to be other sterols, the types that keep us healthy. Oysters, it turns out, can help lower triglycerides and LDL and VLDL cholesterols (the bad ones); moreover, they can help increase HDL, the good cholesterol. Now, if a pharmaceutical company had such a pill, wouldn't you buy it (and add to the company's profits)? And we all know that pills from the pharmacy cost more than oysters and they aren't as fun to eat.

Oysters contain mostly lean protein; just a bit of carbohydrate in the form of glycogen (the starch that makes them a tad sweet), and a bit of fat, mostly unsaturated, for flavor... so a complete food. The National Heart, Blood, and Lung Institute suggests oysters as an ideal food for inclusion in a low cholesterol diet. Many diets rightly recommend high protein intake to stay slim, energized, and keep muscles toned, but the best sources of protein are animal foods, which means lots of the bad fat, the saturated kind that fills our arteries and results in strokes and heart attacks. Sea creatures, on the other hand, don't have much saturated fat but are rich in the good kind of fat, the unsaturated fat found also in plant foods like olive oil, which reduces blood pressure and cholesterol. In addition, unsaturated fats keep us feeling full on less food, as fat triggers the small intestine to send the "I am full" message to the brain.

One more word on omega-3, the fat that does so much good for us, including regulating hormones, reducing inflammation, lubricating joints, and building a strong brain and eyes. There are many claims and studies asserting that the intake of one gram per day of omega-3 (which means eating a dozen oysters) can greatly improve function of the immune system and cut the risk of heart attack as much as in half. Wow.

THE CASANOVA EFFECT

I wrote above of two reasons (pleasure and nutrition) to eat oysters. Throughout history there has been a third reason: sex. I suppose, though, that sex can be considered both a source of pleasure and nutrition of sorts. The notion that oysters are an aphrodisiac is legendary. In Greek mythology, when Aphrodite, the goddess of love, emerged from the sea, she emerged on an oyster shell. And then she gave birth to Eros, the god of intimate, erotic, romantic love. Thus the aphrodisiac connotation.

The Roman emperors believed in it. Why do you think they paid a fortune for oysters, including having some shipped to Rome from Cancale, France?! Those Greeks and Romans got a lot right, so few have questioned their belief in oysters. Certainly not Giacomo Casanova, the paragon of promiscuous lovers, who reportedly ate fifty to sixty raw oysters a day, with a dozen for breakfast being a restorative. (By the way, some people believe raw oysters are a great hangover remedy, providing lots of B_{12}, zinc, dopamine. and electrolytes, as well as protein, to quickly recharge oneself.)

Casanova was something else. In his memoirs he confessed to seducing a total of 122 women in his native Italy, in Paris where he lived, and in Europe where he traveled. He had one novel suggestion for how to eat an oyster: "I placed the shell on the edge of her lips and after a good deal of laughing, she sucked in the oyster, which she held between her lips. I instantly recovered it by placing my lips on hers."

There is not yet compelling scientific proof of oysters' aphrodisiac powers, but there is an often-cited 2005 American-Italian scientific study that discovered that oysters are rich in two kinds of amino acids associated with increased levels of sex hormones. In addition, oysters are especially rich in zinc, which aids in the production of testosterone. So, who knows? But what I do know is that an idea is a powerful stimulant. So if you believe raw oysters are an aphrodisiac, then that thought, accompanied by a few juicy raw oysters, may well stimulate the libido. Amen.

3

MEET THE OYSTERS, AND THE PARISIANS' LOVE FOR THEM

Let us consider again the court of Louis XIV, the Sun King, the ne plus ultra of French opulence and grandeur, the arbiter of French taste for generations of the wealthy...a renowned image and symbol of *La France*. It doesn't get more French than that, does it?

Well, besides appreciating good wit, King Louis XIV loved oysters. He loved them so much, he had them sent almost daily by horseback from Cancale, in Brittany, down to Versailles or his palace in Paris.

He loved oysters to the extent that he is reported to have eaten six dozen at times *before* a meal. (Well, Balzac could eat ten dozen straight.)

"Louie" loved them so much that when a basket arrived late for a lunch, the Prince of Condé's steward fell on his sword.

He loved green oysters from the Marennes-Oléron. He loved oysters cool and raw, but his personal physicians advised him to eat them cooked, for fear on warmer days he would accidentally eat one that had spoiled along the hot journey from the sea and become ill.

He loved oysters with wine. And, no doubt, the king of France often drank the king of wines with his oysters: Champagne. As king, like his brethren, he was crowned in the cathedral in Reims, the capital of the Champagne region, and the bubbly grape from eastern France flowed in the royal court. As Champagne was no stranger to the courts and kings of France, neither were oysters. Louis XIV's grandfather, Henry IV, was a known aficionado of these bivalves.

Oysters and Champagne, a glorious marriage made in heaven. Yet a marriage that is democratic in that many people can now consume these items just as the richest kings of France have. (Today a glass or two of NV Champagne and a dozen oysters cost less than many a pair of sneakers.) *Merci.*

Oysters, though, have curiously been at times the food of the poor and the food of the elite, of the starving and of the gourmets.

Oysters have been around since the times of the dinosaurs, and eating them stretches back into prehistory and ranges across continents and social classes. Charles Dickens in *The Pickwick Papers* describes oysters as food for the poor, yet oysters were staples at Roman feasts and in seventeenth-century European feasts.

The discoverers of America found native oysters in abundance. And along the East, West, and Gulf Coasts, oysters were widely consumed through the nineteenth century—town after town had its oyster lunchrooms, saloons, bars, parlors, and, of course, outdoor stalls. I am happy to note that oysters are making a big American comeback in the twenty-first century.

The Union Oyster House, a famous oyster restaurant in Boston that has been in continuous operation since 1826, has an interesting French connection. Many famous people have eaten there, dating back to the influential Senator Daniel Webster, a regular known to routinely devour plate after plate of the bivalves.

The building that houses the Union Oyster House (originating as the Atwood & Bacon Oyster House upon opening), now a national historic landmark, was built around 1704. Before becoming a restaurant, the building housed a dress shop on its ground floor and a printer-publisher on the second floor. It was on the second floor, above the dress shop and dry-goods stores, where in 1796 and 1797 the self-exiled aristocrat and future (and last) king of France, Louis Philippe, lived and taught French.

Gulp

It took courage the first time I ate an oyster...and I remember it, as the saying goes, as if it were yesterday. I was eleven, and Alice, my godmother, invited me to spend the Christmas season school break with her and her husband in Strasbourg, where they were living at the time. Alice deserves a full treatment as she shaped my life in so many ways, but suffice it here to say she was a privileged woman from a bygone era of a type and class beyond my family's and was quite a character. Spoiled by her father...then by her husband...and charmingly oblivious to it all.

A gorgeous blonde with blue eyes, she was fairly well educated for her time (though no college for her) via private tutors and exposure to all sorts of activities only the rich could afford. Her widowed father never remarried and spent lots of his time and energy as well as money to ensure that his only daughter got the best life could offer, especially during the rough times in between the two World Wars when she was growing up. She was both a gourmet and a *gourmande*. What mattered most to her was food, fashion, friends, reading, music, gardening, and traveling...and her husband, whose practice as an engineer took them to various cities in France for extended periods.

As a young girl, I loved spending time with Alice, my fairy of a godmother who had no children of her own. The first oyster experience was followed by many repeat performances during winter Sundays in Strasbourg, usually starting around the *vacances de la Toussaint* (All Saints' Day) and ending at the close of Easter vacation, the perfect period for oysters. Alice and her husband lived in a cozy apartment filled with light in the old and charming part of town. The pleasant half-hour walk to the center offered a true picture of Alsace with its old houses and stork nests as well as the typical architecture that featured facade windowsills filled with ever-sturdy red-and-pink geraniums. The two of us would go on our morning walk to the cathedral and then buy dessert at the local patisserie while her husband was home cooking. He'd welcome us with the sound of a cork popping and a neatly set table with a white linen tablecloth and a huge platter of oysters (*huîtres* is the word in French, pronounced "weetr") he had shucked.

I was always experiencing new things with Alice, but *What does one do with these little slimy things?* I remember thinking the first time I saw them. So, as told by my mother, when in doubt, always watch the hostess: Alice looked at the oysters with big wide eyes and a smile on her face. She put nothing on them, took the first one with a small fork, detached it from the nerve, and put it in her mouth. Another big smile. Happiness on her face. She then swallowed the juice without a word, looked at me, and said: "You are going to drink the salt of life…from the sea!" For someone who had never yet seen or drank the sea, my puzzled look said it all, but in a second of courage I tried… and wow. It was like nothing I had ever tasted—cool, briny, and almost voluptuously (not that I knew the word at the time) meaty on my tongue. *Oh là là.*

For that eleven-year-old girl, the dozen felt just fine, and that's the portion I like to have to this day. Alice was a bit greedier. Her husband would prepare chicken paillard or veal scaloppine as a main course for the two of us, while Alice's main course was a second dozen oysters. She claimed that Sunday lunch in the winter months was her favorite meal.

Régis, the male protagonist of this book (oysters are protandrous—sequential hermaphrodites going from male to female, and I, a mere woman, bear only XX chromosomes), had his first oyster when he was four or five at his home in Jarnac, in the heart of the Cognac region.

Love affairs and dreams can start early, and often go in a little box somewhere in our heads. Someday, years or decades later, they resurface. This is what happened to Régis. When his father first served oysters, little Régis did not care for their visual aspect. Icky. His father, like so many French fathers (or mothers), said, "Goûte, s'il te plait" (Please, taste), and he did taste. He so loved the "thing," particularly the juice, that he kept asking his father, "When are you buying oysters?"

They were not the food of farmers on a daily, weekly, or even monthly basis! But the kid kept asking, and occasionally the treat would be on the dinner table. Mostly they were a Sunday treat.

A few years later, Régis and his friends would pick up the small oysters along the sea and waterways. They were wild ones, a bit like the very rare *pousses en claires* today. He recalls that as a teenager he was once in a nightclub in the lovely city of Royan in the Charente region, known for its seafront and corniche. His friend and his spouse, whose father was in the oyster business, were with him, and he said, "One day I'll have an oyster place of my own." Dreams do come true, and in forty years his did.

In 2004 he opened Huîtrerie Régis in the heart of Saint Germain-des-Prés, Paris sixth arrondissement. A life-changing decision: often eighteen-hour days, six days a week. No weekends. Passion a must.

His love of oysters is today almost an addiction or obsession. Now that his dream has come true, he eats them almost daily and claims to never tire of them and to be *un gros mangeur* (a big eater). He believes his love has to do with his childhood and love for the sea near where he lived. He finds it remarkable that oysters are a natural product of the sea and claims the magic of each oyster still fascinates him. He loves the texture of the oyster and the taste of the sea. He chides me if I leave the muscle (hard to remove with the oyster fork, and he recommends using a knife so not to leave it). Indeed, passion in abundance.

KISSING THE SEA

If in ancient times all roads led to Rome, it is very safe to say that for the past few hundred years, all French roads have led to Paris. And on those roads from the sea, oysters travel every day.

France is the number one consumer of oysters in Europe, and 90 percent of the production of European oysters comes from France: that's about 130,000 tons, though in some recent years problems (natural and man-made) have caused production to fall to as low as 80,000 tons.

From the English Channel to the Méditerranée along the whole Atlantic coast, France equals oyster farming. From the north, Normandy, counterclockwise west to north and south Brittany, down to Charente-Maritime (Marennes–Oléron and Île de Ré), to the Arcachon basin near Bordeaux, and across to the Thau lagoon in the southwestern Languedoc-Roussillon region are the prime breeding grounds for France's oysters.

The tastes are all different, though the variety of oysters is not. They are mostly (98 percent) cupped oysters, or *creuses* (pronounced "krØuz"), along with some flat ones, or *plates* (pronounced "platt"), mostly from Brittany. These two types, which I discuss in much more detail later, are the common types found the world over.

The breeding methods are many: in deep water, on tables or basins, and in estuaries. However, on more than 3,000 hectares (more than 7,000 acres) between the Seudre and the Oléron Island, oysters benefit from particular methods of *affinage* (aging, refining, finishing) and breeding in *claires* (clay basins). Located below the level of the highest tides, the basins fill and empty on the whim of the ocean. Since the basins are not deep, exposure to the sun allows for a quick growth of plankton, the oyster's food.

The basins used to be salt marshes but have been progressively used for oyster breeding since the nineteenth century. It was Victor Coste at the time of Napoléon III and the Second Empire, who, at the behest of the ministry of agriculture, was asked to come up with consistent and sustainable production methods to meet consumer demands. He compared the methods for capturing and breeding oysters and became the founding father of modern oyster culture by creating the oyster farm system. He recognized the superiority of raising and cleansing oysters in basins and, through legislature, supported the concept of a collective group of basins being recognized as a farm.

The basin of Arcachon and Marennes–Oléron are the only two significant areas in France where oysters reproduce naturally. They provide the spats (oyster larvae) that are sent to many basins elsewhere in France. After having been "capted" on *collecteurs* (tubes), the oyster larvae develop for a year before they are detached to be put in beds, where the oysters will stay for two years. The basin passage gives the oysters their more pronounced *goût du terroir* in addition to the sea savor. Those oysters are also meatier.

While the deep-sea oysters of Normandy are marked by their iodized flavors, and those of Arcachon can be distinctively suggestive of vegetables and minerals or in places citrusy, the oysters of two areas generally stand out for reasons beyond just taste.

In Brittany, where most of the flat oysters are farmed, those from Cancale are famed and have been exported since Roman times. Here the oysters are subjected to some of the strongest and widest ranges of tides in the world and become richly oxygenated and salty and associated with iodized flavors. Even more famous are those from the Aven-Belon appellation (yes, oysters in France have regulated origins). These rare Belons (the species is *Ostrea edulis*) are matured in a site where the freshwater from streams and rivers mixes with seawater and the local algae. They are relatively small, plump, and firm and burst with bold flavors, notably metallic and earthy. Copper is a common flavor description, and Belons have a strong aftertaste of zinc. I appreciate that might not sound so appetizing, but trust their high prices as testament to their gastronomic delights.

The other standout appellation is Marennes–Oléron, which is France's and the world's most extensive oyster farming region. Here the oysters are cup shelled, originating in Japan (species *Crassostrea gigas*), and exhibit a range of briny flavors, from which each basin (*claire*) contributes its unique properties, in some cases even bluish-green dyed highlights from certain algae. The Gillardeau oysters, a brand named after the family that has owned and operated a small company for more than a century, for example, are today grown in Normandy and Ireland but finished in their traditional *claires* near where the Charente River meets the ocean. They are appreciated for their abundant flesh, modest salinity, near sweetness, nuttiness, and strong aftertaste.

These are the oysters that travel to the markets, bistros, and oyster bars of Paris. Parisians love their oysters.

My first restaurant experience of eating an oyster occurred in Paris when I was a young professional right out of college. It was at Brasserie Lipp. And it was on a date. Oysters and romance (read "sex") have long been associated, as I noted earlier. Remember Botticelli's naked Venus rising up on an oyster shell? Frenchmen and French culture just accept the legend of oysters as an aphrodisiac (believing so must mentally make it so?). And Brasserie Lipp has a few romantic atmospherics of its own. As you may know, it is the famous Left Bank Alsatian brasserie dating from the 1880s with a 1920s Art Nouveau interior that is now government protected to preserve the same look. So, physically, it is much the same as when Simone de Beauvoir and Jean-Paul Sartre dined there regularly, the same as when Hemingway wrote there, the same as when I was "romanced" there, and the same as when, in the 1950s, Albert Camus, Jean Genet, Marc Chagall, Balthus, Françoise Sagan, Charles Trenet, and Simone Signoret with Yves Montand were among the artists, celebrities, and politicians who frequented the place. A dozen oysters, umm...

I was also frequently taken to La Coupole, where I remember best the oysters on the *plateau de fruits de mer* (a platter of assorted fresh and cooked shellfish). That I remember the seafood on a platter more than the guys who took me there surely says something about me... or maybe about them! La Coupole, another grand Art Deco palace, was also an artist hangout in its heyday... Pablo Picasso, Man Ray, Brassaï, Albert Camus, Henry Miller, Josephine Baker... ate and drank there... oysters for sure. The *fruits de mer* platter made for a special date and always a special occasion—oysters, clams, shrimp, crabs, crayfish, lobsters, periwinkles, mussels, snails, sea urchins, all on a bed of ice on an enormous platter raised above the table. A little lemon, perhaps a mignonette sauce, some special cutlery, some good bread and butter, Champagne, beer, or white wine. It was a wonderful experience, in Paris or elsewhere, but for me it will always epitomize a slice of Paris. And many Parisians celebrate their joie de vivre at La Coupole and its sister bistros and brasseries. Early in our marriage, Edward and I celebrated a memorable New Year's Eve there. It was indeed romantic—the Christmas and New Year's colors and decorations, sybaritic oysters laid out like the sea, the Art Deco setting that brought us into a movie scene replayed for decades amid the Réveillon revelers and lovers; indeed, the smartly dressed diners all around us that evening kissing and laughing and kissing some more and enjoying the best of moments; the waiters running about in their black-and-white attire, and, of course, the sound of Champagne corks popping, popping, popping.

While oysters are raised and enjoyed all over the world, in Paris—ah, Paris—the oysters are oh so French. Previously mentioned Ernest Hemingway perhaps best captured in English the shared experience of eating a French oyster in Paris when he was living there in the 1920s: "As I ate the oysters with their strong taste of the sea and their faint metallic taste that the cold white wine washed away, leaving only the sea taste and the succulent texture," he wrote in a now-famous passage from *A Moveable Feast*, "and as I drank their cold liquid from each shell and washed it down with the crisp taste of wine, I lost the empty feeling and began to be happy and to make plans."

I have felt the same…in Paris at Le Dôme, the great and classic brasserie; at L'Ecailler du Bistrot; at Garnier; at the historic and touristy Le Procope; at Gérard Depardieu's L'Ecaille de la Fontaine; at Brasserie Lipp and La Coupole; and at *beaucoup de* bistros and restaurants. And I have felt that way dozens and dozens of times (as in a dozen oysters dozens of times) at Huîtrerie Régis, the now supremely regarded little destination and just the place to lose that empty feeling and be happy.

4

A Spring Sunday Lunch a Year Later

It's 1:30 p.m. and some of the first service regulars are about to leave, though Alain tells the young Russian couple who inquire about Régis that he is a bit late but should arrive any minute. (Alain opens oysters at an amazing rate, and you won't ever find any shell scraps when you taste your oysters.) Alain told us afterward that every time the Russian couple come to Paris, they head first to Régis, sometimes directly from the airport.

Alain is about the same size as Régis, which means in France neither notably big nor little, and he likes to stay in the background literally and figuratively. He stands behind the counter near the window and focuses on his job—well, most of the time. His hair is curly and his face that of a child still marveling at people and things. His big brown eyes are alive and tell that he loves life and laughter. When he shucks oysters, which he has been doing for most of his adulthood, he concentrates and does a great job. He even competed in and won some of the famous yearly contests of speed—about a dozen a minute is world-class—though he finds racing outrageous because when one works on speed one can't present perfect oysters without little pieces of shell or grit to the customer. Over the years, he's helped Régis by stepping into the front of the house, multitasking and sometimes setting the tables and taking orders when the student waitresses are late. He, too, has a good heart and puts up with Régis, though he claims he loves his job because Régis has been accommodating, allowing him to do what other employers don't—that is, take two days off at a time during the busy weekend once or twice a month to see his son in La Rochelle. When Alain is away, Régis shucks the oysters, another thing most employers would not do.

We are seated at the one little table for two against the northern wall. Edward, with his bright blue eyes, long eyelashes, and blond-now-white mustache, has the seat with the view of the "ocean" and can't help noticing the restaurant across the street named Le Café des Fous (a double entendre meaning a café for crazy ones, whether the owners or the customers). We are on a small street of passionate people who take their work seriously, but do not take themselves seriously. But fast-forward: Le Café des Fous is no more. Its lease was purchased by a Chinese businessman who opened a Japanese restaurant. Now that's crazy!

When Régis arrives on this beautifully sunny mid-April Sunday, the eight seats outside are filled...with sun worshippers and smokers. Two Frenchwomen of a certain age who sit inside finishing their oysters spot Régis coming out of his blue camionette van, and the mother of seventy-plus years says laughingly to her daughter, "Le pape arrive" (The pope arrives).

It's a fairly typical Sunday with mostly French regulars, except for the Russian couple, probably in their midthirties, who love oysters, sea urchins, and shrimp...not to mention the *assiette de saucisson* to start and Régis's apple tart (he has two slices) to finish (and the woman takes photos of her man eating them). There is also a young Asian girl who is savoring every bite of her dozen oysters with sheer delight, looking at their fatty bodies, comparing *fines de claires spéciales* no. 2 with no. 3, drinking the juice with a big smile, and washing it down with a glass of Sancerre. She is clearly in another blissful world, a zen-like culinary heaven. Now if a photo captured that moment, it could be titled *Eating with Pleasure*.

When the great chefs in France make the rounds of their dining rooms, usually late in the service, it is in the form of a grand promenade. The doyens genuflect, and the friends and eager regulars share *bons mots*. When Régis enters the dining area, his presence simply fills every space of the small room. When he is in the mood, which is often, he goes and greets those who are on a first-name basis, and there are always some. Today and always, as soon as he drops off his apple tart trays and removes his jacket, he goes around and kisses the willing ladies—right cheek, left cheek, Parisian-style. The mother and daughter are about to leave and he offers them a slice of apple tart. They hesitate, but the *gourmande* mother thinks again and says, "Let's split one," and they do. Seeing them eat the dessert transports me to many such shared experiences I had with my mother. It's a special moment. No word is said, but the enjoyment of those three bites of apple tart make for a blissful culinary moment and shared memory. If the pope has his audience, King Régis has his court. He knows his court, and he knew the two ladies would enjoy his tart even more than his oysters.

After his approach to his regulars, he shares a comment or two at each table, usually something funny, but his attention to each customer's words is astounding. Here is a man who rates A++ for attention span and listening skills. He smiles a lot, showing his attractive dimples. He is in a good, or shall we say exceptional mood this day, though admitting that he "finished" at 4 to 5 a.m. this morning (which means he probably went out with his pals for a few drinks) and made his tarts a bit late, at around 11 a.m., thus his delayed arrival.

When he comes to our table I can't help asking—albeit with humor—if he is really the daily baker, and he turns serious and his answer is simple but straight: "Oui, je suis un homme de parole" (Yes, I am a man of my word). His word is his bond.

PASSING BY ON A SUNDAY WINTER'S EVE

After eating elsewhere, Edward and I are heading back home around 10:30 p.m. and take a path that crosses the doorstep of Huîtrerie Régis. The place is packed. Régis sees us and gesticulates. He has been talking to a French couple. He comes outside and says hello. It is a chilly night, but there are two Frenchmen sitting outside at one of the little tables. There are no heaters at all outside Régis. They have their coats and scarves on, and their table is filled with oysters and what is presumably their second bottle of wine, Sancerre, *bien sûr*. Régis introduces us to these characters. We then proceed to laugh for the next fifteen minutes. Two of which are with Régis before he returns to his indoor customers.

Alain comes outside and goes for a quick smoke in front of the building next door. A Pakistani man selling single-stemmed wrapped roses comes by, and he and Alain engage in conversation...and conversation...and conversation. Customers are wondering about their food, no doubt. The conversation breaks up, and the flower vendor goes into the restaurant and manages to sell a rose to the guy Régis is talking to for the woman at the table. On his way back, Alain stops to say hello to us, as we are still standing outside, and for a quick banter with the two men. We could not help saying to him, "That was some conversation," as we look inside at the flower vendor. "He had questions," we are told cryptically.

He leaves and I ask the guys, "So why do you come here?"

"It is close to home," they say jokingly.

C'est tout, but not really.

5

EATING AN OYSTER (FIRST, OPEN IT)

It is after 3 p.m., and Edward and I are up to the fabulous apple tart and down to our last sip of wine when two French girls poke their heads in the door of Huîtrerie Régis and ask, "What kind of oysters do you have?" Alain, the oyster shucker, mentions the eight varieties they have that day. "No Gillardeau?" they ask, mentioning a quality type and producer. "No, the same…or better," he says. True. They ask if they can have lunch. "No," he says in French, "too late." I look at him, amused, as I've seen him work well past 4 p.m. on Sunday afternoons, but he volunteers: "You could not please these two anyway. Trying to impress with the one name they know. I bet they would not know the difference between *fines de claires* and *spéciales*." I got it: they had offended him, suggesting his oysters were not as good as Gillardeau, so his ego and pride asserted itself and he reacted not like a snob but like a wounded child. *C'est la vie.*

Here's the difference.

Types and Sizes

About 50 percent of all oysters grown and served in France come from the Marennes–Oléron basin, what might be called France's oyster basket, or *bourriche*. And about half of all the oysters consumed in France are eaten over a month of year-end holidays.

There is no place on earth, it appears to me, that regulates, inspects, classifies, and details food and wine products more than France, a world capital for bureaucracy, sometimes to the good of the consumer. There are only four types of cupped oysters (again, known in the market as *huître creuse* or simply *creuse*) certified in France:

1. *Fine de claire*
2. *Fine de claire verte*
3. *Spéciale de claire*
4. *Pousse en claire*

N. B. Belons are a fifth type of classified oyster, but, as noted earlier, they are flat oysters and come mostly from Brittany. *C'est tout.* Five types of oysters on the menu, but thousands of different tastes resulting from the locations in which they are raised and finished by hundreds of producers.

Fine de claire and *Fine de claire verte* (green): These two types are similar, though the green are relatively rare. Harvested in winter, the *fines de claires vertes* take their color from the blue-green seaweed in the *claires* (basins) where the oysters are matured. Both types spend one or two months (twenty-eight days minimum) finishing in a *claire*. Three kilos of these oysters (about twenty oysters) are permitted per square meter of *claire*, where they breathe and filter through their gills about two liters of seawater an hour, or as much as twenty-five gallons a day, picking up the particular characteristics of their *terroir*, their pond and its nutrients and microenvironment. They have a relatively soft, not-so-fleshy consistency (the green can sometimes be a tad firmer), along with an attractive marine aroma and a balanced and distinctive flavor. The green can also be a bit sweeter and bear the "red label" seal of regulated quality.

Spéciale de claire: These are individually preselected by eye and hand for having round shells with a deeper cavity capable of housing a fleshier body. They generally spend two to four months growing in their ponds in more rarefied company of only about ten companions per square meter. The *spéciales de claires* taste meatier, with sweetness predominating over saltiness on the palate. Their pronounced flavor is long on one's palate.

Pousse en claire: Top of the line, rare, and in demand each winter, these oysters also bear the red-label designation to inform and protect the consumer. They live a rarefied life, with only one to a maximum of five companions per square meter, while growing for a minimum of four months but commonly six or eight months in their little ponds. They get hand treatment from selection to packing. They are firm and bitable, and beyond the aromas and flavors of the region display a pronounced *goût du terroir*, sweetness, and extra-long finish.

The *spéciales* and *fines de claires* account for the great majority of the production (about 24,000 tons out of 25,000); the *fines de claires vertes* add up to barely 1 ton; and the *pousses en claires* are exceptionally rare, with only 200 kilos marketed per year.

Belons: As I have described earlier, these tend to have a smooth, flat belly and are not finished in *claires* but are *affinées* (refined) in an estuary of the Belon River in Brittany. Their bold seaweed-and-metallic flavor bursts on the palate, and their long finish is somewhat iodized.

When you choose an oyster in Paris, whether at an oyster bar, a restaurant, or in a market or from a sidewalk vendor, besides the type of oyster you choose, you choose the size. France being France, there is a classification system with five categories. Based upon weight, and especially the size and outer dimensions of the shell, the categories are marked with numbers from 0 to 5, with 0 being the largest and 5 the smallest. But just as in our supersized world, clothes may be sized as XL, XXL, XXXL, and beyond, sizings also exist now for the largest oysters. The size designations of 0, 00, 000, and 0000 are applied notably to flat oysters (*plates*), such as Belons (oysters sized 0000 weigh more than 126 grams). When ordering, though, it is still common to revert to the informal practice of asking for small, medium, or large oysters.

THE NOT-SO-GENTLE ART OF OPENING AN OYSTER

Have you ever opened a can of paint by inserting a screwdriver into the cover rim slot and then leveraging and twisting the screwdriver till the lid popped open? *Et voilà.* You know how to open an oyster...that is how you do it, except you use an oyster knife, which is short—only a couple of inches—and wider than a screwdriver and tapered to a point but not sharp. French guys like Régis can pull their Swiss Army–style knives out of their pockets and use the three-inch blade as a substitute. Don't be daunted. Women tend to approach oyster opening like popping a Champagne cork (with timidity), but once they've practiced, it becomes second nature. A trick is to wear a pair of kitchen or work gloves with rubberized palms so you can grip the usually sharp oyster shells firmly and also not worry about slipping and getting jabbed by the knife. Some people prefer a thick dish towel folded in one's hand or held flat on a countertop for protection. *Chacun son goût* (Each to their own taste).

Each oyster has its own "hole," its indentation near where the upper and lower shells are hinged. Find it, and the rest is mechanical.

Using your less-dominant hand, grip the oyster with the flat side of the shell facing up, cupped side down (to better retain the juice). Using your other hand for the knife, and while keeping the blade flat and parallel to the shell, slide the tip of the oyster knife into the hinge joint at the end of the oyster. Work the blade into the hinge, twisting until you feel a release signaling that the ligament that keeps the shell closed has been breached.

With the blade still inserted and parallel to the shell, draw the knife across the interior of the top shell, separating the oyster flesh from the shell. Pry off the top shell and discard.

Your oyster meat should be whole within a small pool of liquid (called the liquor) in the bottom shell. Taking care not to spill the liquor or pierce the flesh, edge the blade under the oyster meat and slide through the muscles attaching it to the shell. *C'est tout.* Nowadays there are any number of videos on the Web demonstrating the knack of opening an oyster.

If you should spill a bit of the liquor when you open your

oysters, let the oysters sit for a while on a bed of ice or cold seaweed, and the oysters will themselves excrete more liquid. This second water is much appreciated by connoisseurs. A dry oyster is not one to eat, and in a restaurant you should consider returning it for a replacement.

MORE TIPS AND SOME CAUTIONS

If you are worried about eating a bad oyster, remember, it should first be alive. If the shell is open, tap it with the oyster knife, and if it closes, all is well. If not, discard the dead oyster. Also, if you have doubts, once you open the shell, if you just touch the oyster firmly with the tip of the knife, it will react if it is alive. And, naturally, if you come across an oyster that just does not smell right, it probably is not right, so pass on it.

When I grew up, there was the famous rule of eating oysters only in months ending in *r*, essentially fall and winter. That was mostly about refrigeration, but not completely. It did not matter if you had a good home or a restaurant refrigerator, summer temperatures, unrefrigerated wagons and vans, and ice that had a tendency to melt, as Louis XIV's physician worried about, all led to dead oysters. That is no longer the problem in the developed world. I have eaten French oysters with delight in Abu Dhabi and in Beijing without hesitation and without consequences.

Oysters need to be maintained at a cool but not freezing

temperature; however, today there is a chance that oysters can become frozen. Then, either they revive a bit after being thawed from their suspended state (if they weren't frozen like a rock); or they don't revive, and you get to eat dead oysters that were frozen fresh and so are not unsafe, just not as tasty. The ideal is to eat an oyster not more than four or five days after it has come from its native waters. (Okay, the ideal might be to eat it immediately, shoreside, as it comes from the water.)

In a French home, oysters are often bought in a *bourriche* (again, crate or basket), and all the pertinent information is required to appear on the basket label, from origin to type to size to date harvested. While you can keep the oysters in the refrigerator, it is not the best place for more than a day because it has a built-in dehumidifier. Oysters will keep nicely for several days in a cool place (5–10 degrees Celsius or 41–50 degrees Fahrenheit is fine). Store them on the concave side of the shell to help the oysters keep their water.

Oysters are fairly safe creatures to transport, because when those two shells close, the oyster inside is hermetically sealed, keeping out all things bad, like bacteria. A bad oyster is rare in France, but I avoid oysters from countries or places with warm waters or polluted rivers and estuaries. My stomach is just not prepared for those local bacteria. Cooking these oysters helps, and cooking oysters in a special preparation is sometimes a signature of a top chef and oh so yummy, too. I address cooking oysters and provide recipes in chapter 12.

I said that while temperature mostly has dictated our preference for eating oysters in months ending in *r*, we know today they can be enjoyed year-round. However, they do not taste the same year-round. In France's warmer months, oysters generally reproduce as well as eat differently, as flora and fauna available to them change with the season, so they taste a little different than in winter and tend to be a bit more milky.

In Preparation for Eating: The Anticipation, Then the Tasting

Oyster lovers like oysters prepared just about any way, cooked or raw, but...the strongest advocates and devotees often argue that the best way to experience and enjoy an oyster is *nature*, naked: an oyster on a half shell with nothing on it. Then you will experience the unique tastes and textures of the specific oyster, its type and its *terroir*.

The most common accoutrement to oysters is just a squirt of fresh lemon on top; that's how Edward eats them. And while I do sometimes eat them *nature* or with some lemon, I am a bit of a maverick and belong to a small minority who prefer oysters on the half shell with some freshly ground white or black pepper, something I learned back in my college years in Paris from a roommate from central France who put pepper on just about everything. I don't, but with oysters...I like it. For me, it helps intensify the flavor of the oyster. (The website lecomptoirdespoivres.com, which sells the greatest pepper varieties in the world, recommends several white peppers to season oysters.)

In France and in many other countries, you can expect a classic shallot vinegar mignonette sauce to be served in a small dish for those who want a little added drizzled flavor (it's not for me). In America and elsewhere you can always count on a hot red sauce or a bottle of Tabasco sauce for those who want to "kick the flavor up a notch," just the thing I do with fresh pepper on some milder tasting oysters. Also in France, a platter of oysters normally comes accompanied by rye bread and salted butter (for the bread).

Rye bread is a classic, as it marries well with the iodine savor of the oyster, plus it is rich in fiber and helps ensure a quick satiety. But with the wide variety of oysters, a country bread or a whole wheat or five-grain type will work as well. As for butter, a Charentais will opt for a Poitou-Charentes type; whereas in Brittany it will be *demi-sel*, or slightly salted butter; and in Normandy it will be a sweet type of butter made at the farm.

6

RÉGIS

Twiggy Sanders, a Frenchwoman from Toulouse who for decades with her husband has owned and operated the *fromagerie* (cheese store) in the Marché Saint-Germain where Régis buys his butter and cheese, has known Régis since he opened Huîtrerie Régis two hundred yards from her shop. She tosses off two quick stories about Régis and his women friends.

"I used to stop by to drop off Murielle, an elderly lady who was a sculptor and lived on rue de Tournon. I used to check in on her daily. She loved oysters, so I would leave her regularly in Régis's care for her treat and would pick her up later. She adored Régis. One can't be indifferent to Régis. He is *un personnage*. Very *attachant* [again, likable and engaging]."

Twiggy, *un petit bout de femme*, a tiny woman, vivacious, energetic, and always in a good mood, explains that after seeing him around the neighborhood and at her shop, their friendship grew through encounters at J'go in the Marché Saint-Germain, a popular modern Gascon café-brasserie that is known for its good southwestern food in generous portions. The owners are from Twiggy's home province, Gers, and she goes there with her husband, daughter, and mother-in-law, particularly on Sundays when the morning market closes late and they are ready for late lunch. "I feel like I am among friends, and my circle there often includes Régis," Twiggy says.

"I like to spend time with him, although I know nothing of his private life (except that he is divorced), not even where he lives, although it's not in the center of Paris and involves quite a daily commute with his truck." She adds, "I know that sometimes he takes a taxi back late at night.

"He is very discreet, which I respect," she continues, "yet he tells me his adventures in travel and love and has plenty of amusing anecdotes. He talks highly of his longtime friend Martine. She has a clothing shop, and awhile back she had serious health issues and was at the hospital. When her friends could not work for her, Régis did. He went to sell shirts! Would you believe this? That's Régis. He'll do anything to help friends.

I know that if I'd call him for help tomorrow, he'd come and sell cheese. Very big heart in friendship."

THE BEGINNINGS

Régis is in his late fifties and wasn't always in the oyster business, but started in the auto business. He was born in Jarnac, in the heart of the Cognac region, to a Périgord father and a Charente mother. He had a happy childhood growing up between the Charente and Dordogne regions, with grandparents who were farmers in nearby Limousin. His maternal grandmother had a great influence upon him and gave him a sense of responsibility. She was a true *maîtresse de maison*, and during World War I was left alone to handle the farm and the rearing of three children. She would get up at 3 a.m. to sell at the market in nearby Angoulême. Her food was what we would call today *bio* or organic. Régis has delicious memories of her *pintade* (guinea fowl) recipes (thus he loves Jacques Brel's song about the "pintade du Périgord") and her wonderfully traditional, simple home cooking. She was also a great baker and made him cherry clafoutis, which he makes, using her recipe, for his *huîtrerie* during the short cherry season just before he closes for the summer.

Early on in life, he became a great nature lover, and walking is his favorite hobby. Today he likes to trek in the mountains and spends a few weeks each summer in the Alps. The Atlas mountain range in Morocco has of late become an obsession, so much so that he took a three-week excursion there with a few pals last summer. Just talking about it makes him salivate. What a way to escape.

School for him, though, was "academic"; not too strong in French he confesses. He was not the best of students, but was liked by his teachers for the same reasons his customers like him today. At the end of his last school term, the principal said to his father, "He is okay. He can do something else; school is not for him."

That was okay because for this man of passions—women, hiking, oysters—an early passion was cars and being a mechanic. After a summer at the farm, he found a job for a year as a mechanic, then went on to get his CAP (certificat d'aptitude professionnelle) after two years of study.

One day, a friend took him to see a car race, and he saw an ad with an invitation to "become a mechanic for racing cars," and that was it. He applied, got the job, and for some years was part of a Renault Formula One team. Next he decided to open his own shop, which led him to selling Alfa Romeos. That period lasted about fifteen years, and toward the end he bought an auto-parts firm and a few years later he sold it. By then, he certainly had acquired customer and sales skills…and a long list of contacts, many of which he maintains to this day.

But he still had that siren's call to oysters, and an idea for his kind of oyster bar, that had been percolating for years. He acquired his oyster knowledge via his mentor, Jean Maurice

Garnier, an oyster breeder in Mornac-sur-Seudre. And with that anchor affixed, he began to test his idea by setting up an oyster counter outside a friend's restaurant in Levallois, just outside Paris. It was enough of a trial investment to tell him he was on the right track.

He wanted to create something different. *Vive la différence.* Yes, there were plenty of good places to eat oysters in Paris, including some big establishments with big names, but he was disappointed by the large brasseries, the places running on numbers, turnover, where the customer was a mere number. More often than not, he found the oysters full of grit, which means they were shucked by someone who had not been trained, or trained properly, or who had to open so many that there was not time for perfection. He wanted, like so many passionate people, to create an atmosphere that was not an atmosphere as defined in books, but a personalized ambience built around the customer and giving him or her the best he could. He wanted his customers to feel like the food and service were coming from the heart, his heart (his romantic trait). He has always believed the customer is right in general, though some can be unpleasant (read impatient), and for that type, his little gem of an oyster shack is not welcoming. Yet a restaurant with fourteen seats and a couple of outside tables cannot accommodate many people. And in his definition of a good restaurant is the statement "It's one which is not for everyone," and he leaves it at that. No further comment... except: *Et c'est bien.* And it's good.

Régis's concept of being great versus good, or his "best" (we all have our definitions), is first illustrated in his use of the best ingredients—from oysters, wines, butter (*beurre demi-sel cru à la baratte de bois* [salted hand-churned butter] from Pascal Beillevaire, made with raw cream and Noirmoutier salt), and bread made by the Alsatian bakery Kayser, to the one dessert made by himself every day (following, as I have noted, his grandmother's apple tart recipe most of the season and, toward the end, a spring fruit-of-the-week clafoutis). If there are leftovers of things like dessert and bread, they are never kept for tomorrow, as he gives the food to friends and business neighbors on the little street. He also sets the tone with white linen tablecloths, real napkins, beautiful dishes, and nice silverware; and, a few years into the business, he learned about the importance of glassware and is excited to get new wineglasses.

He also picked a professional and experienced *écailler*, or oyster shucker, the previously mentioned Alain, with almost twenty years of experience. Alain trained and worked in the top Paris oyster establishments on the Right Bank, mostly the seventeenth, sixteenth, and eighth arrondissements. While Régis was testing the competition, he and Alain met, and the two indeed have a good and trusting working relationship and share the same passion and respect for the oyster. Their personalities sometimes clash, but that's another story!

As one friend shared, "Régis is charismatic, protective, wants to please, and, yes, he can be *coléreux* [irascible]. Don't go there when it happens. Don't try to mediate. You have to know how to *le caresser dans le bon sens du poil* [rub him the right way]. When things don't go his way, he'll fight. Nothing scares him. I have seen him in action."

I return to my refrain: The French love oysters, and Parisians adore them. Régis's place was an immediate success.

He has lots of regulars and an international clientele. Of course, Parisians come from all over the city—some are writers, businesspeople, actors and celebrities, gourmets and gourmands, and restaurant owners and chefs (Madame Lasserre is a regular, as is the famous chef Alain Dutournier). Like the Russian couple mentioned earlier, one Spanish customer gives him a call when he lands in Roissy and comes directly to the restaurant, even though there is a no-reservations policy, but just to make sure that he'll be expected no matter the wait!

Just about every afternoon toward the end of lunch service, a Pakistani newspaperman comes in selling *Libération* and also *Le Monde*. The guy is an intriguing character himself who has written a book, and for sure he knows what he is doing showing up at the time he does; otherwise, no doubt Régis would have read him the riot act and he would not have become part of the family and the daily drama.

His greeting to the staff as he comes in is "Bonjour, les enfants," an old French phrase that shows familiarity with French culture as well as humor, especially since the staff and most of the clients are older than him except for the lunch waitress.

When asked what he thinks of Régis, he replies without thinking a second, "This man is not into making money, he is a *bosseur*, a hard worker; his place is nice and clean, his staff pro, and his customers real connoisseurs."

The oyster shucker smiles and offers him an espresso. "Don't you like oysters?" I ask.

"Yes, when they offer me some, I eat them." He laughs, and after selling a few papers to the locals, some of them regulars he recognizes, including one elderly lady who is a weekday fixture with her dozen oysters and a glass of Sancerre, he leaves with an "Au revoir, m'sieurs-dames."

RÉGIS'S TEMPER

Régis has an enemy, his credit card machine. They constantly fight it seems. One day he was in a foul mood because his card machine did not work through the lunchtime service. After a few back-and-forths with the company, someone showed up to fix the device and connections. New batteries and all. Solved for now. At the dinner service, the first customer asked for his bill and the next episode began. The machine didn't work and wouldn't work. Seeing the filled room and the upcoming disaster, his fuse got lit. He went around the counter with the machine and, in front of the crowded customers, he threw the machine to the floor and stomped on it again and again. It just took a few seconds, and no one said a word, including Régis. Apparently understanding and agreeing, many of the customers got up and helped him destroy the thing. What he must have had to deal with to have it replaced is another story, but that's Régis.

A year or so later, he sees a lady he recognizes with some guests. She is an American who speaks in French, and he goes to her table and greets her. She opens her wallet and takes out a tiny blue piece of plastic and shows it to him with "Vous étiez un peu énervé ce soir là" (You were a bit upset that evening). He laughed and sent a complimentary bottle of wine to her table.

Women

I have come to think of Régis in regard to oysters as akin to what Azzedine Alaia is in regard to fashion: *le maître absolu*, best described as a reference—no fashion show, but a few trunk shows, no compromise, total integrity, an attitude, and did I mention even a bad temper at times. If Alaia knows how to dress women, Régis knows how to feed them. One pushes the door and enters their universe. Some are welcome, some not so much, and a few not at all. One must know how to speak to them. He certainly knows how to speak to women.

Régis, something of what is known as a man's man, clearly loves women, pretty women. In love, when he was young, he must have been *un coeur d'artichaut* (someone who falls in love with every girl he meets), Twiggy says. "Now he is a bit tamed because he is getting older. I've met some of his ex-girlfriends, who were all beautiful women.

"He makes us laugh a lot, especially with tales of his amorous adventures," Twiggy adds. "He sometimes gets carried away and tells such intimate details that I can't help exclaiming *'Pas possible!'* [Not possible!], amid spasms of laughter. But I know he is telling the truth. You cannot make up such details."

When I tell Twiggy that a female regular once said to me that Régis was likable as a perfect friend or lover, but as a husband, "non, jamais, never," Twiggy paused and said she would agree with this woman's opinion.

7

TASTING AN OYSTER (AND TALES OF OYSTER VIRGINS!)

As with many of the finer things in life, such as music, paint-
ing, and wine, there is an approach to the experience of tasting an oyster and then looking back upon the experience that
translates to "I don't know much about X, but I know what
I like." That's fine. Not cerebral but holistic and visceral.
You will know if you like oysters or not once you taste a few.
Such an approach and attitude are based upon your subjective
response to the experience of eating or drinking or listening or
viewing a work of art or nature (often the combination of the

two). With each experience, though, you bring more to the next experience, and that often translates into evolving likes and dislikes. Want to learn about wine? Taste a lot of wines. Want to learn about oysters? Taste a variety.

Of course there is another approach to the experience of art and nature that attempts to formularize the approach and even the terms so that you can bring more to the experience and theoretically take more away from it. Or at least take different things away. So with wine, tasters commonly analyze the tasting experience by looking at the color of the wine, smelling its "nose," and then tasting it and analyzing its flavors. We try to describe them with equivalencies (we learn words like *tannic* and *dark fruit*); then we note the finish or aftertaste, how long and pleasantly it stays with you. Much the same holds true for tasting an oyster.

The physical process of eating an oyster is simple: bring the shell up to and parallel with your mouth, and with a small oyster fork, slide the oyster into your mouth and then slurp in the juice from the shell. Or, just as commonly, you can simply tilt the shell and slurp the oyster and its juice into your mouth. Next, you chew it two or three times, so that the flavor explodes onto your palate, then swallow the entire oyster.

In an oyster bar or a restaurant and at home, your platter of oysters should be accompanied by a moist towel—now mostly a commercial packet containing a moist towelette—or even an old-fashioned finger bowl with water and lemon, so you can clean your fingers after (or before) touching the shells and oysters. Nice and necessary little hygienic touch.

Like tasting wine, there is a process for more formally approaching the experience of tasting an oyster. Here is how I see it as a variation of look, smell, taste, and follow-up.

Starting with the oyster already on its half shell, the **look**, the appearance, can tell you the size and type, but you will also note color, from translucent to pearl-like to green around the gills to blue-green. You will also note if the oyster is plump and smooth or perhaps flat. All of these are okay. They are identifiers and differentiators and help you pick what you like.

The **smell**, the **odor**, or the **aroma** (a word with better connotations than *odor* or *smell*) of an oyster is a treat. You are smelling the sea in its various flavors and intensities, depending on where the oyster comes from. The smell should be superfresh; its power can be mild to strong. When I am in Paris and I smell an oyster, I can be transported, Proust-like, to the seaside far away and back to a childhood or adult experience.

Salinity is a telling characteristic of an oyster, and it appears on the nose and on the palate. It can be mild or strong and in some cases powerfully iodized. All salts do not taste the same.

On the palate, some of the operative **taste** words are *crisp, mild, briny, buttery, sweet, milky, nutty, earthy, grassy, fruity, citrusy, watermelony, melony, creamy, clammy, clean,* and *bright.* But here words are insufficient to describe the myriad of subtle flavor overtones that come from each oyster's habitat, its *terroir*, and there are so, so many. Also, note how the flavors change on the palate, perhaps from initial saltiness (but what kind of salty?) after the first bite to a sweetness (what kind of sweetness?). And, just as the second sip and impression of a wine is influenced by the first and can be different, the taste of a second oyster is subtly different from the first, and you can perhaps pick up new or differently modulated flavors.

The **texture** is telling as well: *soft, crunchy, chewy, bitable, smooth, watery, firm, hard, airy,* or *creamy.*

The **finish** or **aftertaste** brings a great deal of the satisfaction experienced from the taste of an oyster. And, again just like wine, the longer the finish, the better. The minerals and fats in the oyster reveal themselves in the finish, as do evolving and lasting flavors. The more complexity, as with wine, all the more telling and often more satisfying.

The Dance of the Virgins

Ah, that first bite. "He was a bold man that first ate an oyster," Jonathan Swift is quoted as saying. Indeed.

It seems most people, like Régis and me, remember eating their first oyster as clearly as they remember the first time they...but not my husband, Edward. He grew up where there were clams and oysters to be picked, and he remembers eating clams on the half shell at clambakes and gatherings when he was very little and assumes some of those clams eventually were oysters. If someone would open the shells for him, he ate and drank what was inside. Some people never change.

I asked a number of Parisian and other friends about their first oysters. Here are their recollections:

Annick, a Parisian with roots in Brittany: My first time was when I was ten. A rich client of my father, a sugar entrepreneur who had married a modest Brittany woman born in Carantec, would come each year for a short stay. Eventually he settled there for retirement. He was *dingue* (crazy) about oysters and would send us a *bourriche* or invite us to his home to eat oysters. And my father, who, alas, was not the type to love anything, not even the sea(!), loved oysters. Astonishing. He was a man all introverted who did not express himself much (shy, tormented, the opposite of a bon vivant, the exact opposite of my mother...), yet could not find words strong enough to declare his love for oysters. I remember being horrified as a small child hearing him say at the table: "I'd eat them on a dead man's head!"...Horrible. I was outraged...and disgusted!

I had to try them. My dad declared he did not know how to open them, which is indeed more than simple, so it fell to my mother to open the carton's worth of oysters. I found the texture disgusting. If my parents liked the stuff, perfect. They could keep them!

I can't tell you how my disgust grew when I realized the beasts were . . . alive.

My hope each time we would visit our friends was that they'd serve a platter with *bigorneaux* (periwinkles), shrimp, and crayfish. Total happiness. Little fleshy beasts, firm and cooked!

I finally grew up. And I came to know oysters little by little with friends. I even had a Gallic boyfriend, funny, gourmand, generous, who loved to cook and share joyously with friends. He would open dozens of oysters with such happiness and speed, a glass of white wine next to him, and suddenly I associated oysters with a happy feast. We would go and get the oysters from chez Morvan in Carantec, and we would come back driving like mad and make a beautiful platter. I'd buy lots of lemons, which are still my favorite accompaniment. But since then I've learned that freshly ground pepper also enhances the taste of oysters.

However, my strongest memory (in my mouth) of tasting them was in Paris, at the Hélène Darroze restaurant, with my friend Mireille, ha-ha. I don't recall the exact preparation, but it was sumptuous. The impression was of eating the sea. (It was an oyster with green apple aspic, osetra caviar, with an "iced" cream of duck foie gras, and rye breadcrumbs.)

★   ★   ★

Michèle, a Parisian: I married a great oyster lover and now have two teenagers; the eldest loves oysters almost as much as his father, but he was only willing to try them at age twelve.

My first experience was at my in-laws'. For our engagement! My family didn't care for oysters. I had never had any before. I am still a new convert...I eat six, the least fat ones. I like them alive, very fresh, with a drop of lemon juice.

For me they are still for festive occasions. I like their silver color, which marries so well to dishes, silverware, beautiful glasses, tablecloth, and candles. It's the easiest festive dinner to prepare (I am not the shucker!), and it amuses me to see guests sometimes eating with their fingers.

My husband, the great amateur, likes them without *tralala* (fuss). He buys two dozen almost every Sunday during the *r* months for him and his son. My daughter and I make crepes.

I love eating oysters at the great Parisian brasseries with my lover (husband). We order a huge seafood platter; he devours almost all the oysters; I pretend to see nothing. We have the impression of taking advantage of our beautiful city.

Diane, a Brit who lived in Paris for a few years: My first experience of oysters? Well, actually it's very easy to recall, since the opportunity to indulge came late in life. It was January 28, 2011, and I was forty! I had not long since made the leap from the UK to France and was staying with a friend's parents in Nogent-sur-Marne. They informed me that from about November to February, their apartment overlooked an oyster seller. And sure enough, as we were in January, several times a week the Oyster Man (as he became known) would set out his fine selection and I would watch curiously from the window, drawn by "Huîtres d'Oléron" written in neon above his stall in the street below. My friend's mother, already a mentor in many things French and culinary, loves oysters but never buys them because my friend's father doesn't like them, so she rarely has anyone to share the moment with. As I had never tried them, I was happy to volunteer.

As we approached the stall on a crisp winter's eve, the first thing that amazed me was the choice. I had naively thought that there were—just oysters! Apparently the Oyster Man asked (my friend's mother translated) which variety we would like and what size. We followed his recommendation as my friend's mother revealed to him that it was to be for my very first experience of oysters. (I think I may have blushed, especially when he gave me a look as if to say, "What, at your age?" *Pfff, les Anglais!*)

Back in the warmth of the apartment, there was a bustle of activity to open the oysters and prepare for the ceremony. A table was laid, napkins were selected, also lemon, vinegar, followed by bread and, of course, wine. (Unfortunately, I was too excited by the oysters to remember the wine!—*pfff, les Anglais!*) Then, preparations complete, the moment had arrived. Following a brief instruction and demonstration from my friend's mother, I began with a plain oyster: nothing else.

My first reaction: pleasantly surprised! I swallowed, oyster, juice, the lot. I hadn't really known what to expect, but I liked it. And I remember that the more I had, the more I liked them! I experimented a little, trying lemon, vinegar, pepper, but (maybe it's because I'm British, the island influence and being connected with the sea) in the end, I loved them plain. Just oysters. We shared the platter equally between us until, alas, they were all gone.

But not quite. I congratulate myself to have had the forethought to have saved the shell, complete with lid, of my very first oyster. One of life's precious souvenirs, which now adds a splash of the sea to my home.

Stéphanie, an American and longtime resident of Paris: My first memory of oysters was at Felix's Oyster Bar in New Orleans, Louisiana, at the age of four or five years with my father. According to the story, he set me on the bar (in my little pink frilly dress), where the shuckers fed me oysters one after the other. They seemed amazed, even in New Orleans, an oyster city, that a little girl of this age should have such an appetite for oysters! My sister and mother detested these creatures, so it wasn't a family obligation. Strange but true, I am a born oyster lover.

I like them raw and *nature*—mainly without lemon juice

or shallot/red wine sauce, which for me is the only way to dress up a less-than-superfresh oyster. A slight sprinkle of freshly ground white pepper is perhaps the only justifiable "artifice." Some warm versions (if not overcooked) can be delicious, but I still prefer them raw.

"Close your eyes and open your mouth!" Voilà, my advice to the novice who has never tasted an oyster.

Na, a Moroccan who lives in New York: My first? In Oualidia (Morocco) in an oyster park in 2004. I was with my friend Miriam, who converted me almost immediately. I ended up eating two dozen. It was a very beautiful gastronomic experience. Happiness!

I like them alive, raw out of the shell, with or without lemon; and I try to encourage virgins by preparing a slice of country bread, buttered, and placing the oyster on top with a drizzle of lemon. It is easier to eat and get used to the taste. I also insist on the fact that oysters are good for health and loaded with vitamins.

My strongest memory is when I had just met a man. He discovered I love oysters. He surprised me that very evening by delivering a wicker basket with four dozen oysters and a love note. He had completed the round-trip to Oualidia to make sure they were fresh.

I also remember when I was in Dakhla, in the south/ Moroccan desert. Dakhla is known for its giant oysters. We rented a boat and headed to discovery. A few hours later, the motorboat driver, a local from Dakhla, takes us to a hidden spot for lunch. We land and swim to this little shack where the fisherman/oyster farmer welcomes us with a glass of mint tea, and while we sip our tea he goes to take his oyster baskets/cages from the sea. He makes us taste them just out of the water, and then makes an oyster tajine with olive oil, garlic, cumin, paprika, parsley, coriander, and saffron and some Moroccan bread. We ate on the sand in the middle of nowhere.

Carmen, an American raised in Puerto Rico: My first experience was when I was seven or eight, back in the small town of Boqueron on the west coast of the island in Puerto Rico. There was only one kind—they were sold by the fishermen on wooden tables built on the sand next to their boats. I think they were 5 cents each.

I like them both ways, raw and cooked. To me, if I am eating them raw, I like just a touch of lemon or piquant sauce (made from Puerto Rican hot peppers) like we had when growing up. If cooked, I like them coated with a panko mix, with a touch of red pepper flakes to spice it up a little bit. I love to drink cider or Champagne with oysters, but my first choice is beer.

I have a lingering memory of diving for them. I was ten—there is nothing like diving for oysters (lobster, conch, etc.), then sitting either on the boat or the beach shore shucking and eating them.

★   ★   ★

Dorothy, an American and multidecade New Yorker: I was probably nine years old, in 1960, when I tasted my first oyster. I lived in Tallahassee, Florida, then, and it was the segregated South. My dad taught at an all-black university, Florida A&M. Restaurants were segregated, too, and we were even not welcome in many stores. Still, we had a very vibrant life, and I remember being under the impression that black people made the best fried foods ever—fried chicken, fried seafood, especially fried oysters, which is the only way my family ate them.

On special weekends, Dad would load us into our station wagon, a Plymouth, and we'd drive to Apalachicola, in the Florida panhandle, south of Tallahassee. Some summers, we'd rent cottages near there with other families from the university. But most of the time, we'd drive up to what was pretty much a shack, a small "restaurant" on the side of the road, where women and guys in white aprons would fry the most delightfully light fish, shrimp, oysters, and hush puppies. They'd drain them on brown paper bags and serve them with coleslaw and cheese grits and lighter-than-air biscuits with honey and butter. Sometimes I'd sit on a stool and watch them dredge the oysters in cornmeal, so I knew what "naked" oysters looked like, but I'd never eaten one until that day when I was nine.

I was a tomboy and loved helping Dad clean fish and do stuff like that. (He wasn't a great fisherman, but he loved the outdoors and the time it gave him to think.) I loved his company. So I jumped at his invitation to go fishing with him. He was a tall guy, 6 foot 2 inches, and he'd walk out on this thin spit of rocks, way out into the water, which I think may have been Apalachicola Bay, which was fed by the Gulf of Mexico. I'd watch cranes fish, and fish jump, and sometimes I'd catch hermit crabs. On other occasions, when the whole family came along, we'd crab from a bridge, dropping nets baited with mullet heads into the water, and pull up delicious blue crabs. Once, when I was about ten, we raced a few across the kitchen floor and then grew afraid to pick them up!

Anyway, as it got late, I sat in a shallow little cul-de-sac watching my dad start to pack up and move closer to land. I'd been eyeing these large shells that had attached themselves to some rocks when I realized that they looked just like the oyster shells that were strewn over the parking area. So I took a knife that Dad had left in a toolbox, pried one off a rock, and then opened it. And there it was, this gleaming, plump organism that smelled of the ocean and salt. It was suddenly irresistible. So I slurped it into my mouth and held it there for a few seconds, getting the sense of it, probing it with my tongue. As I was chewing it with I'm sure a most beatific look on my face and a wet chin from its fragrant juices, my dad rushed over with a horrified look on his face. "You shouldn't have done that," he said, not unkindly, just with concern. "It might have diseases, bacteria." Frankly, I didn't care. I was hooked. But he did shoot me worried glances on our way home. It wasn't until many years later that I learned that oysters from this area were quite famous!

I have never had a preparation that I didn't like, but I prefer them cool, not ice-cold. I think the taste is muted if they're too cold, much like most white wines. If I can't have them raw on the half shell, my second-favorite way to have them is fried because of the memories I associate with that preparation, and because, very important, John, my husband, and the girls will eat them fried.

Guillemette (and **Simone**), Parisians: I certainly was too small to remember my first. I adore them but detest preparing them, so I love them when they are served to me. The only exception was fried-and-breaded oysters in New Orleans. The taste got a bit lost. My best ever, though, were eaten in New York at Momofuku...served with green mango!

I have a lot of family memories of eating oysters, moments when men go to the kitchen, generally complaining about the tools ("Your oyster knife is *nul*").

My best memory, however, is of my little daughter, turning around an oyster plate. I said to my friend Anne, "She is only eighteen months, it may be a tad young,"...and hop, Simone took one and adored it.

8

Mr. Oyster Purveyor

The trip from Paris to the oysterland of Marennes–Oléron takes about four and a half hours via the highway, traveling at or close to the speed limit of 130 kph. I suggested to Edward that we make the trip so I could visit the Oyster Museum in Marennes and absorb a little of the culture up close. Plus, we could stay at the seaside resort of Royan and visit the historic, touristic, and commercial center of Saintes. He agreed, and I took charge of making the car rental reservation, as he was busy traveling for business when we made the decision.

Though we had stopped off in the area before, mostly for meals, going to or coming from Bordeaux or Cognac over the years, we had not experienced the Roman and medieval cathedral towns of the area or quietly smelled the sea and seen the boats that recalled the rustic Cape Cod and Nantucket of my high school year abroad. Here is colorful, low-key tourism at its best...*la France profonde.* Apart from the boring drive along the highway, I recommend the visit. I mentioned the 130 kph speed limit because two months after my return to Paris, I received a souvenir of the journey in the mail: a speeding ticket with a fine of 180 euros. In France, there are now speed cameras in certain locations that take a photo of your license plate when you exceed the speed limit. Edward did all the driving. The car was rented in my name. We weren't rushing. I got the souvenir of my first speeding ticket (actually I got two). He laughed.

The museum was fun and informative...and quick. Plan for thirty minutes. Built into the saltwater marshes, the Aventure de l'Huître (www.cite-huitre.com) is a series of five huts in which, through audiovisuals, old photos, and re-creations with antiques, is traced nicely the history of the oyster industry, the workers, the farming technique, the oysters, and the ecosystem of the Marennes basin. There is even an oyster bar if your appetite is stimulated. Plus, the *écailler* will teach you in two minutes or less how to open an oyster.

VIVE LA DIFFÉRENCE

I love Burgundy wine. But there is good and there is great... there is Vosne-Romanée and there is La Tâche. And there are

Burgundies made by such esteemed winegrowers and wine-makers as Christophe Roumier and Dominique Lafon. Great Burgundies are works of nature, soils, and microclimates (collectively called *terroir*), and of vignerons and winemakers. Much the same can be said for oysters. When it comes to cupped oysters (*creuses*) the Marennes-Oléron family name and their company, Gillardeau, as previously noted, are quality references. You just don't eat a *spéciale* no. 2, you want to experience a Gillardeau *spéciale* no. 2.

Planning my visit to oyster country, I asked Régis where I should go. "Papin-Poget," he began. In his inimitable way, Régis had tasted his way through the Marennes-Oléron basin producers and settled on Papin-Poget as being the best purveyor of *creuses*. I can say I have never tasted better, and Papin-Poget oysters are a far cry from what one can find at some of the more commercial brasseries and markets. There is Burgundy and then there is Burgundy.

Régis is a loyal follower of these oysters and oystermen. And he works at maintaining a strong personal relationship with all his suppliers and makes periodic visits to see them. His idea of a day off (Mondays, when Huîtrerie Régis is closed) is driving down to the Charente on a Sunday night, sleeping at his sister's, then saying hello to as many people as he can on Monday, which includes, for example, a woman he has shared only a few words with and who, say, works in an isolated office on the second floor up a back stairs and clears orders.

I wanted to meet the family Papin-Poget.

PAPIN

Yves Papin, who is in his sixties, likes to introduce himself by stating that he became an oyster lover while wearing a bib. As a three-year-old he was given his first oyster to taste, and it was apparently love at first taste. The rest is the recent history of a first-rate *ostréiculteur* or *parqueur* (as an oyster grower is sometimes called; as oyster-growing pond areas are called parks). He claims he did the same with his three daughters, though for the girls the oysters had to be cut up into small morsels. As for his métier of *ostréiculteur*, he likes to say that he was born in the marshes with his *cuissardes* (high boots that cover the thighs) on. He is a man who works hard and beams joie de vivre. He knows his profession inside and out and is able to help at any stage of the oyster's life and route to the table.

Monsieur Papin gets very excited (his eyes shine and the smile on his pink cheeks reminds me of a kid opening Christmas presents) talking about oysters, and one can see his passion without a blink. He also likes to compare oysters to wines (another passion). The notion of *terroir*, of *cru*, of opening them, eating them, tasting them. An abundance of analogies.

He does not get tired of eating the "pearls," as he likes to call them, any time of the day or year, though there are some special and obligatory moments like Christmas and New Year's Eve, birthdays, vacationing in the mountains, hosting meals at home, and...and...and. The pleasure factor comes first when serving oysters to start a meal, he argues. Like a bottle of Champagne, a platter of fresh oysters always connotes pleasure and eating them confirms it. When pressed to elaborate more on "Why do you love oysters?" He adds the "aesthetic" element: "It's a noble food so wonderful on the table, and it beats *carottes rapées* [grated carrots]." Who will argue? "Eating oysters," he says, "makes you dream...of nature, the sea, vacation, and more; the sky is the limit."

He is also very proud to be in the Marennes-Oléron basin, which has a unique ecosystem. Many oyster farmers, such as Papin, have *parcs* in Normandy because of the area's richness in phytoplankton. Later the oysters are brought to Poitou-Charentes for the *affinage*, which will give them the appellation "Marennes-Oléron." *Affinage*, as noted earlier, is the last stage in raising oysters and is unique to the Marennes-Oléron basin. With the goal of improving the quality of the oysters, they are placed in basins/pools (*claires*) for at least a month and up to six months, where the oysters fatten up and their branches turn greenish, thanks to the presence of a green algae.

When the popular notion that oysters are an aphrodisiac comes up, he says mischievously, "I suppose women are the ones who would know if they are." Papin has great respect for women in his life and field and claims the notoriety of oysters is the work of women like his grandmother. He undoubtedly grew up hearing many stories at the kitchen table. The stuff of Sunday lunches.

His grandmother was what was then called a *femme de cabane*, which meant she used to be in charge of selling oysters before modern transportation and distribution existed. The work was quite a sacrifice for the family, as the wife would take off with the kids to spend the selling season—in those days, September to March—living in a sort of shack in cities like Angers or Arras and go door-to-door to the bourgeois homes to sell oysters from their *bourriches* (in this instance very large wicker baskets containing up to 84 pounds [35 kilos] of oysters each) shipped by train. Such a yearly voyage was common from 1890 to 1914, while the man stayed at home, literally a widower. Cell phones would have been handy!

On our first meeting he demonstrated the efficiency of the packaging, now partly mechanized with an assembly line that starts with the sorting of the oysters (mostly done by women as a seasonal job) and ends with wrapping the oysters in small wooden crates to be shipped. As one young woman was taking a break, he took over and performed her work until she returned. Team or family work is essential in the business.

The history of the Papin firm started with Yves's grandfather, who was a *parqueur* who owned a few *parcs* and did some fishing. So did his father. Yves started to work at the age of fourteen. He has strong memories of the disaster of 1965, with the first *claires* replacing the flat oysters of the old days.

NATURE INTERVENES

Here I want to point out two important things. First, oystermen are farmers and frequently face challenges wrought by nature. From year to year, relative disaster can hit. And second, the oysters that are grown in the Marennes-Oléron, indeed anywhere in France, are not from the same family of oysters rushed to the table of Louis XIV.

The indigenous flat European oysters (*Ostrea edulis*) that the Romans and the French kings ate virtually disappeared from a combination of violent disease and overharvesting. (A tiny percentage survives today, including the famed Belon.) Back in the 1853–59 period, Monsieur Coste addressed maintaining a sustainable oyster supply by developing the current farming tradition. Disease, though, began hitting the flat European oysters especially hard in the 1920s, which led to their being replaced with a cupped species (*Crassostrea angulate*), known as Portuguese oysters. These oysters had been introduced as early as 1860 and seemed resistant to what ailed the European flat oysters. The Portuguese oysters ruled almost exclusively into the 1960s, when they, too, succumbed to disease. Introduced next was the current species found to be immune to the Portuguese and European oysters' problems, the so-called Pacific oysters (*Crassostrea gigas*), which are Japanese in origin but widely cultivated worldwide.

While there have been two epic "oyster plagues," and we are eating the third species to flourish in French waters, year in and year out, farmers of all kinds continue to have numerous worries and encounters with the fickleness of nature and thus some good years and some bad years... and some disaster years. "Nature is a cruel mistress," as the expression goes.

In 2013, many oysters, especially young ones, succumbed to a killer bacteria (for oysters at least), *Vibrio aesturianus*. But what caused the growth of the bacteria is not clear. Nature's turmoil was a likely contributor. Perhaps, people posited, all the rain lowered the salinity of the oyster *claires* for a period, or the intense heat raised the temperatures too high, or...It must be noted, though, that since the 1980s a new variation of oyster has been introduced widely around the world: sterile oysters that grow faster and bigger and are not milky in summer or thin after spawning. By adding an extra chromosome (or two), something that occasionally occurs in nature, the oysters become sterile. *Et voilà.* Diploids become triploids not by genetic modification, but by artificial inducement. However, it appears these triploid sterile oysters have less resistance to disease, especially when young, and contribute to the supply swings.

One thing is sure: oyster prices in France are up.

Sustaining a Family Business

Yves Papin explained that in 2000, Thierry Poget became his partner—a sign of the times and succession planning for the next generation of the *patrimoine*, something taken very seriously in France. Probably the passing of Yves's two daughters had something to do with his planning direction for the next generation. His third daughter was in education, but some years ago decided to quit teaching and come back (apparently a trend, as many young people don't want to stay in the business, but somehow one kid in the family tends to return at thirty to thirty-five years of age to keep the family business going), and now she is part of the team. And so is her husband, Matthieu, who handles direct sales including the market in Angoulême, one of their top spots.

Monsieur Papin is proud to see customers come back again and again, as the name of Papin-Poget is renowned for quality all over France. They sell, however, mostly in the region, with La Rochelle and Angoulême as main markets, as well as a few oyster restaurants in Paris, four oyster bars, and the esteemed Huîtrerie Garnier and Huîtrerie Régis. For now, Yves and Thierry are the decision makers.

The partnership with Poget did not happen overnight, but made sense as the industry is facing competition. Although there are still plenty of small businesses in the Marennes-Oléron region, about twelve hundred, the onetime number of seventy major companies is now down to seven. Modernization and cost-cutting are the major challenges, and consolidation is a survival tactic. The Papin–Poget team of thirty is split between Utah Beach, Normandy, where a dozen grow the *naissans* (baby oysters), and the *claires* and the headquarters (packaging center and a few offices) in Marennes-Oléron. The work has changed, too, with better material, transportation, and distribution systems and less physical labor than in the old days.

Thierry is younger, the first generation of formally educated people with technical expertise going into the business, and also he comes from an oyster family. He brings a different approach to work and to life than those from his father's generation, and Yves listens and likes it. It very much looks like a great father-son working relationship. With three young daughters in school, Thierry thinks balance is part of the game. He also has hobbies beyond work—playing the piano and singing, for example—and he is an avid sportsman, enjoying activities from biking to playing tennis and golf.

MOVIE ACTOR, OYSTER PRODUCER

As I came to meet people in the oyster business, I realized that as in the wine or restaurant business, they seemingly all know one another. Plus, many share similar traits. A class of them are true French characters, with passion, joie de vivre, and a sense of humor as key ingredients in their DNA. For them, *l'art de vivre* means sharing (*la convivialité* is the sacred French word), getting together with friends around a table and eating, drinking, conversing, joking, and laughing, as well as giving back as a way of life and closing the sharing circle. This is a common thread to their eternal youthfulness and love of being and doing what they do, which often means long days, hard work, and lots of challenges, whether dealing with oysters, vines, or people. They love themselves, their lives, and their jobs. Their work is to make a living and a tad more for little extras, but they are not interested in killing themselves 24/7 to get rich and famous or attain status. Their aim in life is to help people dream and to diffuse as much *bonheur* (happiness) as possible into every aspect of their lives.

Joël Dupuch is a good example. He came to know Régis through Twiggy and at the previously mentioned brasserie J'go in the Marché Saint-Germain. He is an oyster farmer, seventh generation, as he points out with pride. But today he is better known, even famous, in France as an actor.

The film director and actor Guillaume Canet (who shares his life with Marion Cotillard and a young son) picked Joël, an untrained but natural actor, for parts in both the 2010 *Les Petits Mouchoirs* (Little White Lies) and the 2013 *Jappeloup*. He was great in the films. As a result, Joël has been interviewed in the local and national French press, and the statements he made (the values he shared) led a French publisher to convince him to write a book, *Sur la Vague du Bonheur* (On Happiness's Wave). Like many people who have published a successful book, he is enjoying the feedback from his readers tremendously. Yet, in his heart and head, he remains an oyster farmer.

Joël's enterprise is in famous Cap Ferret, south of Marennes-Oléron, in the Bassin d'Arcachon. His company is called Les Parcs de l'Impératrice and produces and wholesales oysters, concentrating on the *spéciales*. The challenge with *ostréiculture*, according to Joël, is that it is not an exact science but requires lots of work based on patience, humility, science, savoir faire, and much manipulation. The key to quality obviously has to do with picking the best *parcs* for growth, but as Joël points out, that's just the beginning.

Like many children, he had other dreams in his young life, which took him first to try politics (did not last long... the illusion died fast when he saw the "pollution," he said), and then, at twenty-six, he entered the restaurant business, creating bistros in Paris and all over France. Next, he traveled the world before heading home to get into the family business, a decision he does not regret. "Je vis dans un espace de rêve et vois la vie en rose" (I live in dreamland and see everything through rose-colored glasses).

He heads to Paris almost every Tuesday and spends Wednesdays "feasting" with his pals. He calls these get-together festivities *les fêtes de l'inutile* (useless feasts). He loves them. One of his favorite joints for meeting his Gascon friends, such as chef/restaurateur Alain Dutournier, is Dutournier's Le Carré des Feuillants and Au Trou Gascon especially. He often visits friend Olivier at J'go, and occasionally other restaurants where he sells his oysters, such as the famous Brasserie Lipp, for which he is the exclusive oyster provider. So if you have been there and eaten oysters, you have eaten Joël's.

Joël's friendship with Régis, whom he likes and admires, began over a meal and no doubt a few glasses of wine at J'go. It is not always easy to regulate supply and demand in the oyster business, and with a surge in his business, coinciding with a period of smaller monthly harvests due to a seasonal bout of disease, Régis could not get enough oysters to satisfy his customers. A worry. "I can help you out short-term," Joël told Régis. "Let me ship you some *spéciales* each week." "No, no," said Régis, knowing the generosity of the offer and the shortness of supply throughout Paris at the time, and understanding he would be taking oysters previously destined for other establishments. "Mais oui, mais oui," argued Joël, implicitly saying what are friends for if not to lend help during a rough period. That clincher is something Régis appreciates and practices. "You don't need to mention my name, just sell the oysters," Joël offered. The men shook hands.

The motto of France is "Liberté, égalité, fraternité." These oyster guys certainly know about fraternity.

9

What to Drink with Oysters (Perhaps Sancerre)

I was in the tasting room of a remarkable winery in Provence, Château Romanin, a biodynamic estate carved, cathedral-like, into the stone of the Alpilles hills. I am a fan of their rosé, but I like their reds as well. "What about a taste of white?" the woman behind the tasting counter asked. "No thanks," I said, looking at one of my companions, a man with considerable professional experience with the wines of the southern Rhône and beyond. She said, "The grape is 100 percent rolle...

vermentino in Italian." "What would you eat with it?" I said, partly to be polite but also curious. She and my friend paused for a beat, then said in unison, "Oysters." Wow, now I was really curious.

"Okay, I'll have a taste." Pouring the wine, she said in winespeak, "Low yield, no oak, six months on the lees." The color was clear straw, and the nose suggested almonds and some citrus. This was confirmed on the palate. The minerality of the Alpilles, though, seemed the distinguishing flavor of a nicely balanced, round yet still relatively crisp wine. *Yes, it could go with some oysters,* I thought to myself, *though it would not be my choice.*

A great many wines can marry well with oysters, and by "marry well," I mean contrast or complement in a way that 1 + 1 = 3 as a gastronomic experience, an interesting and rewarding taste exercise. The challenge when ordering a wine to go with your meal of oysters is that there are hundreds of different taste experiences associated with different types of oysters coming from different seaside environments. Whether they are eaten raw or cooked affects the choice of wine to pair with them also. And likewise, there are hundreds of subtle and not-so-subtle different taste experiences associated with wines made from different grapes or from the same grape in a different location.

Here's the good news: you can make choosing a wine as complex or as simple as you want. There are a few tried-and-true pairings that yield remarkably pleasing returns.

Pleasure first. Here are two 99 percent rules:

1. Ninety-nine percent of the wines that go best with oysters are white wines.
2. Ninety-nine percent of the wine choices offered in Paris to go with your oysters will be French wines.

M. F. K. Fisher (the great "poet of the appetites," to use John Updike's phrase), in writing her short memoir-cum-cookbook in California, *Consider the Oyster* (1941), declares a French Chablis, Pouilly-Fuissé, or Champagne—very dry white wines—as the safest match to oysters, especially when the bivalves and the wine are served at the same cool temperature. Her recommendation remains sound and safe. There are dozens of enticing additions that could be made to the list, especially when playing with the fattiness and flavors of different types and origins of oysters.

For me, though, there are six types of French wines that will meet the taste-and-marriage challenge 99 percent of the time and will appear on Parisian wine lists: Champagne, Chablis, Sancerre, Pouilly-Fuissé, muscadet, and Entre-Deux-Mers. And if you don't want wine with your oysters, then sparkling water, sparkling cider, and beer are proven alternatives. It seems bubbles have an affinity with bivalves.

You won't find many non-French wines on wine lists in France; an occasional Italian or American, Spanish or New

Zealand wine, perhaps, or some other country's entry. More for show than tell, but there is little question that oyster-friendly white wines exist the world over, which I discuss in a later chapter.

In the oyster bars and bistros of Paris, not only will you be offered wines by the glass and by the bottle, but commonly there is a house wine or two that will be offered by the pitcher, as in a one-quarter, one-half, or full (750 ml) pitcher. Here you might also find a less-common, low-cost wine that the proprietor believes goes well with oysters.

Champagne: Having spent more than a quarter century in the Champagne business, I know it is the rare person who isn't happy with a glass of Champagne. And I know that Champagne, with its crisp acidity, complex flavors, and dancing bubbles, marries well with oysters and seafood and much, much more. Its strong and bracing backbone stands up and cuts through the pronounced salinity of foods well. It is, of course, the wine of celebrations, and since half of the French oysters are eaten by the French during celebrations, such as Christmas and Réveillon, Champagne is the ne plus ultra festive wine of choice in many homes. It was what we drank in my home. Champagne from the Champagne region, located ninety miles northeast of Paris, comes in varying types and styles, all of which marry well with oysters, and finding out which ones work best for you is a pleasure indeed.

★   ★   ★

Chablis: The suggestion of Chablis with oysters rolls trippingly off the tongue. This dry chardonnay from the northernmost area of Burgundy is a top-of-the-mind suggestion. A famous very dry white wine with a pronounced purity of either minerals or crisp acidic fruits, depending on the limestone soil where the vines are grown, always seems to complement oysters if the wine is well made. There are four levels of certified quality and style in Chablis, starting with Petit Chablis, then Chablis, then Chablis Premier Cru, and finally Chablis Grand Cru, with accompanying increasing prices. When it comes to the great Grands Crus (there are seven), their varying tastes are quite distinctive; however, whether a Chablis comes across as fruity in the apple-lemon vein, or buttery and nutty, or more classically flinty and in the mineral vein, the brisk and refreshing acidity is a winning and time-tested partner to oysters.

Sancerre: When in doubt, this easy-drinking sauvignon blanc from the eastern end of the Loire Valley bordering Burgundy is the safest bet to please most palates. Much of what can be said to be pleasing about Sancerre holds true for Pouilly-Fumé, which is made in the village just across the river from Sancerre. There is a wide variety of flavor overtones to various bottles by different producers or different areas of Sancerre, but all have a vibrant acidity, which is not as assertive as the other wines I am mentioning, and exhibit either a predominant minerality or a floral-fruity nature. The Sancerres are not too citrusy or vegetal, a frequent trait of sauvignon blancs from areas outside France's Loire Valley. A grassy quality to some sauvignon blancs from around the world can mirror the taste and go with some oysters grown outside France; but overall, for me, vegetal accents and oysters are not the best contrasting flavors.

Pouilly-Fuissé: This chardonnay from the Mâconnais region in southern Burgundy is generally a good value in white wine, though it is a large region with a large production that can greatly fluctuate in quality from producer to producer and vintage to vintage. It is characterized by true Burgundy chardonnay flavors, with a good balance of fruit and acidity, but with a touch of minerality. For three times the price, you can move up into the Côte de Beaune heartland of the great white Burgundies and enjoy a Meursault or Puligny-Montrachet with your oysters to gain more elegance and complexity in the marriage.

Muscadet: Made from the melon de Bourgogne grape in the westernmost Loire Valley region near the city of Nantes, muscadet is a high-volume, modestly priced wine associated with the oysters and shellfish of France's Atlantic coast. It is very dry, with what I find to be an aggressive acidity that cuts through the fattiness of oysters and more. It presents pleasing white flower flavors and some citrus effects. I can go a year or three without a sip, and then I order a glass and always smile and wonder why

I don't sip it with oysters more often. (The answer is that Régis has converted me to a Sancerre follower...and then there is Chablis and always Champagne.) The best known of the four areas of the muscadet appellation and an offering that you will see on wine lists in Paris is Muscadet Sèvre et Maine. Overall, these are good, simple wines—perfect for quaffing with the sea in sight and the sun shining—and when aged *sur lie* (in a vat with the dead yeasts not yet removed), they can pick up a bit more body and mouth feel.

Entre-Deux-Mers: This exclusively white wine from the Bordeaux area has an aromatic palette offering citrus, yellow flowers, and exotic fruit notes. They are soft in the mouth and refreshing. Sauvignon blanc is the chief grape, which gives the wines their perfume without an excess of what the French like to call *nervosité* (edgy on the balance side). When made well, these wines are medium light, balanced, and have a strong aromatic power. Sémillon grapes in the blend complement for roundness, and muscadelles add pleasant musk and wild notes. In general, the French drink their local wine and Champagne. The Bordeaux region is between the Arcachon and Marennes-Oléron basins, so when in Bordeaux, expect Entre-Deux-Mers or a white Graves to be the wine served with oysters.

10

RÉGIS'S FAVORITE WINE

At times, to get a wine conversation going, Edward likes to ask the question "What's your favorite wine?" or "If you could have any wine for your last bottle on earth, what would it be?" I am amazed when some people answer before he has even finished the question. Not Régis. When asked in his *huîtrerie*, the smile fell off his face, and you could almost hear the grinding of his thought machine. He took the question very seriously, even though we were pretty sure what his answer would be. Some people pick a famous and great wine they have never tasted, others an old wine that connects to a year that marks an important event in their lives, and others go back to the greatest wine and wine memory they possess for a repeat performance.

Régis said, "Sancerre." "Well, there is Sancerre and Sancerre," Edward prompted, and Régis's thought machine really went to work. "Plante des Prés from Daniel Crochet," he then added, citing one of the wines on his wine list. He gave a current vintage—no doubt the year will change over time, but the choice of this as his favorite wine won't.

Régis's love for wine grew with his love for oysters. He discovered wines, and more particularly Sancerre, at friends' homes. When it came to creating a wine list for his place, it was a fun little game. He thought there would be few wines, but only the ones he loved and felt his customers would, too, because they were good pairings with his oyster selection. Being a wise guy, he did several blind tastings with friends who knew a thing or two about wine and put his favorite Sancerre brands in the selection: he says Crochet came first and Alphonse Mellot got high marks, then also Jack Pinson as well as those of Jean-Claude Chatelain in Pouilly-Fuissé. Voilà, nearly half of his wine list was complete. Today it is a bigger wine list than the small space can seemingly hold, but that's Régis.

I'd been to wine regions all over the world, and dozens and dozens of wineries, but I had never been to Sancerre. I wanted to meet Crochet and Mellot and visit the source. When I told Régis my idea and asked him for some contact information, he said, "You must go on a Monday and I will meet you there for lunch." That's Régis. He didn't want to miss the fun. Plus, it seems he likes to drive down in his truck, hang out a bit with his friends, and come back loaded with cases of Sancerre. I don't want to know the details.

The trip is a mere hour and a half by car from Paris and perhaps fifty years in time. For this trip, Edward rented the car in his name and drove (sans tickets). When we arrived, I was astonished by the extent to which this area is frozen in time. It was another delightful experience of *la France profonde* and very close to Paris. We stayed in the village next to Sancerre, called Chavignol, just over the hill (but still classified as Sancerre), where the famous Crottin de Chavignol goat cheese is made: picturesque, quaint, rustic, and agricultural, with a more than decent inn and restaurant. Recommended.

Monsieur Mellot

For me the treat always is to put a face on a wine I've been drinking for years, whether in Paris or New York, and Mr. Mellot (senior) was no disappointment, having about the same vivacity and aging capacity as his wines.

With so much of the world becoming similar thanks to globalization, it's always refreshing to see that some things subsist, and some *maisons de vin* (winehouses/domains) continue to follow centuries-old traditions in the same family. Alphonse Mellot, *Vigneron de Père en fils depuis* 1513: yes, this house of winegrowers celebrated its five hundred years in the same family from fathers to sons in November 2013. Alphonse, who calls his son now in charge of making the wine *dieu* (god), is still going strong. He is vital, young late sixties, *un personnage*, a character, though I think he always was and calls himself an anarchist. His professed love of flying—he pilots his own small plane—makes him sound like a twenty-year-old.

He met and welcomed us in the town square (*place*) in Sancerre, a lovely village that really does make one feel that France has not budged in centuries. The pace is slower than in Paris, and there was no rush, though it was already late morning when we arrived. A few people were still lingering over *café* and *tartine* at the square's cafés, while some tourists were already eyeing the lunch menus.

Monsieur Mellot greeted us warmly and with real pleasure and then announced the plan: a couple who owned a wineshop in Paris would join us for a cellar visit and lunch. Régis would join us when he arrived. That happened in short order.

Alphonse Mellot started with a few jokes about Régis, who had brought along a good friend from Paris. Interestingly, Régis was kind of shy next to Alphonse's strong personality. One could note a great sense of respect and deference to the winemaker and a pride in making the introduction. Régis was all smiles and kept telling us how much he liked to come down here and that he felt at home with his pals. It was easy to see it on his face. No doubt they've had lots of parties over the years, and Régis often shows up on Tuesdays for lunch at his oyster place looking a tad tired from too much drinking and eating the previous day and night. Right away one could feel the deep friendship between two artisans passionate about their trade.

Régis's friend looked familiar. He turned out to be someone we'd met at the restaurant who organizes safaris to Africa and has been Régis's friend for thirty years. What I learned was that he is married to Régis's great friend Christiane, who serves lunch at the *huîtrerie* whenever Régis needs help or one of his young lunch *serveuses* can't make it. Christiane is very devoted, and they've known each other since childhood. Both grew up in the same town, Jarnac, in the Charente, and married others but kept in touch through the years. Christiane's lovely daughter, Elodie, worked for Régis at lunch for years while pursuing her dance career, and now has her own school.

Christiane told me one day when she was working, and Régis was not yet back from Sancerre, that Régis is the only *commerçant* she knows who does what pleases him rather than pleasing the customer. Yet he loves to connect and sit down with the customer at the end of a meal and talk and listen. She started by saying how *entier* (how whole, how complete) he is with his integrity, rigor, perfectionism...a rare thing. He is interested in only the best and is uncompromising in that regard to anything or anybody. She vouches for his sublime apple tart, which, no matter how he is feeling, he makes six days a week, nine months a year, knowing all the baking tricks and using the finest butter and organic golden delicious apples. She says, "Il a un fichu caractère," her way of saying he is tough to deal with, as he can show his best and his worst during the course of a service. He easily gets carried away, and his stubbornness is one of a kind. And yet one could see she is in awe and would do anything for Régis.

We go to the cellars, and Alphonse Mellot does not lose a second in pointing out that there are fewer and fewer cellars in the wine world today, as most growers now have little financial choice but to opt for what looks like outdoor barns: cubes with corrugated roofs and some temperature-control system that avoids the extremes.

The Mellot family cellars, though, are the real thing, built underground and showing the rows of aging barrels. He does mention that there are still a few real cellars around, such as Vacheron's, but clearly his family has the best in the area. With 60 hectares of vineyards, and about 45 employees between the vineyards, cellars, and tasting rooms/shops in town, the Mellot rule in Sancerre land and stand as the reference point for quality and professionalism.

The tasting of a dozen wines from barrels in the Mellot cellars took about two hours. To me, all the wines were good and displayed promising and distinctive personalities. The tasting took time because Alphonse Mellot is quite a talker, sometimes even about wine.

We tasted mostly white wines but a few reds. Most people think white when thinking of Sancerre, and the red variety is a small production (20 percent) overall, but they are more and more trendy with a young generation of French people in the know who want to impress their guests or help them discover new varieties.

Burgundy wines they are not, though the grape variety is pinot noir. The soil is more Loire Valley, even though Sancerre is very close to the Burgundy border. Before phylloxera hit in the late nineteenth century, the majority of the wines in Sancerre were red.

Throughout the tasting in the cellars, Alphonse joked and emphasized the importance of *terroir* and put down most Bordeaux wines, which grow on sand and thus are devoid of major characteristics. To him they taste alike and lack personality, except, he said, the Right Bank Saint Emilions and Pomerols.

What is important about the taste characteristics of Sancerre is that there are three different types of soil that produce wines with distinctive differences. There is silex, or flinty clay, which—surprise—tends to produce wines with flinty minerality overshadowing most of the fruit. There is white soil (*terres blanches*), which is chalky clay from fossilized seashell limestone. This is known as Kimmeridgian marl. This soil produces fruity and age-worthy wines. Then there is *caillottes*, gravelly limestone, which results in a more delicate and perfumed wine.

When it comes to describing wines, Alphonse likes to mention how he once had to describe a wine (not his) to a group of journalists, so he pretended to write notes and then recited a ready-made text, written by a famous enologist/sommelier, which described the appearance, nose, taste, and food pairing of a wine that could apply to any or none, and left the group speechless. To him, wine is not about words and lengthy descriptions, but about pleasure, conviviality, and sharing. The rest is nonsense.

When asked what he'd eat with each of his wines, Alphonse was quick to reply, "Tout," anything, but prefers again to talk about the soil structures and always always always wants to share a bottle with *une jolie femme*, a pretty woman. Here goes the Frenchman!

Another few statements he made during the course of the day helped me understand the man and what he stands for: "Aller à l'essentiel" (Whether it's about the wines or life, only the essential matters) and "En France, tout est interdit sauf ce qui n'est pas autorisé" (In France, everything is forbidden except what's not permitted). And when he talked about certain visitors... *les notaires* (a profession in France to negotiate sales of houses, land, etc.), who could be *collants* (uptight) when they first came but always left *la queue entre les jambes* (with the tail between their legs), we all laughed. Mellot cited all sorts of authors amid his jokes.

Since it was a Monday in Sancerre, the best "restaurant" was closed, and after tasting all those wines, we were starving. Monsieur Mellot invited us to lunch in a tiny place in Chavignol. The place was worth seeing, and the owner looked like he was right out of an old movie—a bit roly-poly, with a big red nose and a big grin. The menu was limited, and we opted for the tomato stuffed with fresh goat cheese from Chavignol, *bien sûr*, and then it was a pata negra with tagliatelle, and for dessert a thick chocolate mousse sure to give one energy to walk through steep hills in the afternoon.

The first course came, the owner-waiter added knives to the table setting, and Régis looked at it, stuck his hand in his pocket, came out with his pocket knife, and smiled. Mellot agreed and pulled out and opened his pocket knife. *Where am I?* I thought. *What year is it?* Then Régis's friend pulled out his knife. The guys were happy. We drank more Mellot wines, and Alphonse told the owner he'd bring some bottles to replace whatever we consumed. No bill was given. He probably had an account, and again the trust and friendship came out.

A memorable lunch ended, we split up, and Régis took us to visit the House of Crochet.

THE HOUSE OF CROCHET

Monsieur Crochet is a man in his early thirties, I suspect, who is the portrait of a young vigneron in twenty-first-century France. We arrived at his winery to find out from his young wife that he was out working in the vineyards, but she was ready and happy to drive us to inspect the various vineyard sites, which they lease and farm.

So, driving over hills and a variety of soils, we saw what constituted Crochet's individual bottlings. Along the way, we passed him on his tractor: he was driving through a steeply sloped vineyard, headphones on to cancel the noise, head down, peering at the vines and grapes and his work. Monsieur was working hard, as there were just a few days left to do a lot of the necessary work before the heavy rain forecasted for the following week.

After a nice tour led by his wife, we met up with Daniel at another hillside. Here was another man interested in the soil and talking and showing the young buds and what was next on his agenda. "See that line of trees there...you cannot grow grapes there, the soil is too erosive...and over there it changes from clay to gravel. Here, look at this grape and that one ten feet over there. Completely different." The enthusiasm and passion for the vineyards was apparent, as was a love for being outdoors. He felt lucky to have his job, and his wife and his two young kids. His wife joked that he was not good at administrative work, and his bookkeeping was worse. She was pleased and honored to oblige him and handle all that...and "he is in heaven."

After our multivineyard tour illustrating the differences between higher and lower elevations as well as sun exposure, including hours and angles and a host of defining details in Mother Nature, we headed to Daniel's tasting room for proof that what he was talking about was in the bottles.

It was a nice little tasting room in a nice little winery: nice maps, nice little bar, nice wine descriptions, and wines for sale. We were just into our first swirl, smell, taste, and who showed up? Alphonse Mellot. Then the jokes started flying back and forth like flying saucers...or more like Frisbees. Then the corks really started popping and the laughter was contagious. Edward said he felt like he was in a friendly neighborhood pub or bar.

Régis was eager to tell us about how after the Crochet wines kept winning his blind tastings, he became immediately fond of young Crochet when he placed his first order. Crochet told him, "You pay me when you pay me." That is the kind of trust Régis has in his friends and embraces in others. From that trust the friendship grew, and now it's like they are great old friends meeting, yet they've known each other less than ten years.

There is an expression in the wine business: "Like the

winemaker, like the wine." That's why hospitality is such a big part of the wine-marketing business. It is very hard not to like the Mellot and Crochet families. When I dined recently at Le Vivier, a one-star Michelin restaurant in the Provence village of Isle-sur-la-Sorgue, I was pleasantly surprised to see "Sancerre La Moussière (A. Mellot)" listed. Of course, I just had to order it. Delicious.

11

MORE ROUND SHELLS
'ROUND THE ROUND WORLD

When I was a high school exchange student near Boston, I learned to eat lobster and then more lobsters (addictive), but curiously my host families did not proffer any oysters. No Wellfleets, Chathams, Island Creeks, or Cotuits, to name just a few of the finest oysters found in Massachusetts.

Growing up in Alsace-Lorraine, far from the sea, I did not experience oysters until I was eleven, as I have written; however, thereafter, they were obligatory in my home on New Year's Eve, and when I went to university in Paris and started to work there, oysters were routinely part of my diet. French oysters, while varying widely in subtle tastes based on how and where they were raised, are relatively limited in the types and locations. I had not yet experienced the wide world of oysters, or the wide world, for that matter. I thought oysters were oysters, delicious but basically the same.

Then early in my New York life I visited the Oyster Bar and Restaurant at Grand Central Station, a cavernous landmark that opened in 1913 with the railroad terminal. What oysters...at least twenty-five kinds, none that I had ever heard of and none from France. There were Witch Ducks from Virginia, Sunset Beaches from Washington State, Sister Points from British Columbia, Pemaquids from Maine, Peconic Pearls from Long Island, Malpeques from Prince Edward Island, Lady Chatterleys from Nova Scotia, Belons from Maine, and my soon favorite, Kumamotos from Oregon. Wow, what choices, what shapes, what flavors. My eyes and palate were opened. On each successive visit, there were more choices among the two dozen or so temptations. I even remember experiencing my first oyster from New Zealand there. Some two million oysters cross the plates and the palates at the Oyster Bar each year. That's a hard number to contemplate...averaging more than five thousand *a day.*

London, like New York, is an oyster town rich in history and oyster restaurants. On many a pilgrimage there for theater or libraries with my literary husband, we've found our way to the J. Sheekey Oyster Bar in Covent Garden for some West

Mersea oysters or Maldons from England and an occasional *fine de claire* from France. Or sometimes we've dined not far away on Maiden Lane at the famous Rules, with its oyster origins, and began our meal with a few Wild Cumbrae rocks or Duchy of Cornwall rock oysters.

Closest to our hearts and stomachs, though, are the oysters at Bibendum, located on Fulham Road in South Kensington. I have often stayed in the area and am old enough to remember when the Michelin garage and tire shop closed and then Mr. Conant opened Bibendum. Many a day I have had Colchester rocks, Jersey Royales, and Loch Ryan no. 3s there.

How Many Countries, Let Me Start to Count...

There is indeed much oyster life beyond France, as I have learned from experience and curiosity. Besides America, Canada, and England, there are thriving oyster industries in Ireland, Holland, Spain, Mexico, Morocco, Australia, New Zealand, Chile, Brazil, South Korea, China, Thailand, and Japan, as well as small suppliers in many other countries.

In France, you'll recall, there are generally only two types of oysters: (1) *Crassostrea gigas*, so-called Pacific oysters, the world's most cultivated oyster and the oyster of the Marennes-Oléron, and (2) the *Ostrea edulis*, known as European flats, best represented by and called Belons. They also grow natively in

Maine and Washington State and in northern climes besides in Belon, France. (A third species, *Crassostrea virginicas*, or Atlantic oysters, is among the species cultivated in France in the Étang de Thau, the large lagoon opening into the Mediterranean Sea, whose oysters are called Bouzigues. The small *Ostreola* or *Ostrea conchaphila*, commonly known as the Olympia oyster, is a fourth species that can be found in France, though in very modest quantities.)

There are other species spread around the world. Kumamoto oysters, for example, are their own species, *Crassostrea silamea*. Small and creamy with some melon overtones, they are prized. Atlantic oysters (*Crassostrea virginicas*), mentioned above, are also native to America's northeast coast, including the area in and around New York. The commonly named bluepoints, Malpeques, Wellfleets, and Beausoleils constitute the vast majority of oysters harvested in America. There is no mistaking their briny character and firm, full-bodied flesh.

If you have ever seen oysters smaller than Kumamotos, they are probably *Ostrea lurida* or *Ostrea conchaphila*, Olympia oysters, which can be found in Puget Sound and British Columbia (and in small quantities in France, as mentioned above). These are native American oysters and once populated San Francisco Bay in abundance. They are both sweet and metallic tasting.

The Sydney rock oyster, *Saccostrea glomerata*, the native small to midsize oyster of New South Wales, is among the elite oysters of the world, with intense flavor along buttery and creamy lines.

I want to mention just two more species. First, *Ostrea chilensis*, the Chilean oyster, small, briny, and firm, is, as its name suggests, a native species from Chile. And thus, like oysters from Australia and New Zealand, Chilean oysters are at their peak during Northern Hemisphere summers. And second is Suminoe, *Crassostrea ariakensis*, the Chinese oyster nicknamed Sumo, which is hearty and large and increasingly grown around the world, though I would not try it in China's polluted waters.

In all, scientists have classified about four hundred species of oysters. But no two taste quite the same, of course, not even within the same species, as the flavor is heavily influenced by the habitat, the *terroir*. Even oysters raised under five feet of water could taste different than those raised at seven feet. Minerals, algae/plankton, salinity, tides, and more beyond the species influence their taste.

THE WORLD'S BEST? THE TOP 10?

Taste is subjective and taste preferences are built upon experience, yet we all want a shortcut to finding our favorites and our richest experiences. Thus today's ubiquitous top 10 lists. I doubt anyone has tasted all four hundred species of oysters, and it is impossible to taste the oysters from the thousands and thousands of places where they grow. But as life is too short to waste time tasting tasteless oysters, let the game begin—my first take on ten to try:

1. If it is Monday, for me the best is a *pousse en claire*, the rare top *creuse* from the Marennes...firm and sweet and packed with flavor and length. When it comes from Papin-Poget, all the better.

2. If it is Tuesday, then for me the best is a *Belon* from Brittany with its powerful salty, copper, and algae flavors.

3. Since I am such a Francophile, let me be fair and include a non-French oyster I have yet to taste, but great chefs, well, great Danish chefs, proclaim it probably the best oyster in the world: the *Limfjord oyster*, which comes from the cold waters north of Jutland. These are endangered European flat oysters, similar to flat-shelled Belons and from the same species. Here they grow slowly amid the cold waters in the largest native concentration remaining in Europe (and once monopolized by the king) and reportedly are more meaty and subtle than other oysters and exhibit a nutty character without pronounced iodized sea flavors.

4. Even though some think *Kumamoto oysters*, preferably from America's Pacific Northwest, are not for the sophisticated, I know what I like, and I love them. Their modest size,

their seductive sweetness...umm. With a glass of Chablis or a sauvignon blanc...let the hedonists top that.

5. *Oualidia no. 3s* from Morocco are worth the detour. The pristine pure lagoon (along the coast between Casablanca and Essaouira), washed by the crashing waves of the Atlantic Ocean, is a natural oyster park. Eating the Marennes-Oléron breed of oysters seaside in Oualidia shows why the Oualidia no. 3s are known as the best in Morocco with their clean salt and mild grassy flavors. The French-influenced wine industry in Morocco is mature, and I can testify that among the memorable choices was the CB Initiales, a chardonnay with a few years of bottle age that evokes a fine Burgundy and raises the Oualidia oyster experience to even greater heights.

6. When I flew to Tasmania for business some years back, my gourmet friends said that I must eat the oysters and drink the wines. I remember the wines as being good...but the *Tasmanian oysters*—primarily the Pacific oysters *Crassostrea gigas*—were great and unforgettable: big and buttery, salty and seaweed flavored, clean and crisp. With pinot noir and chardonnay being first among equally great grapes grown here, the sparkling wines produced in Tasmania are indeed sparkling... just the thing for these oysters.

7. What's a trip to Sydney without tasting a few *Sydney rock oysters*? This native Australian oyster (*Saccostrea glomerata*)

is now cultivated widely throughout New South Wales and beyond. I have found the taste to vary—no doubt due to where they were raised—but it is safe to say they are distinctive: smaller than the average oyster, softer and creamier, with varying mineral and iodine flavors. I am looking forward to my next dozen.

8. A few years back I was eating oysters on the half shell in Boston at Barbara Lynch's first great restaurant, No. 9 Park (still going strong sixteen or so years later). I bit into a bivalve that was buttery and salty yet focused and sweet on the finish... wow. I remember involuntarily saying to myself, "I love oysters." That happens now and again, and when it does, I know I have just had a special experience. The oysters were Massachusetts locals: *Island Creeks* from Duxbury Farms. Perhaps I should have listed this as number 9 in honor of the restaurant.

9. The legendary *Galway oyster*, Ireland's native European flat oyster (*Ostrea edulis*) now is mostly cultivated. What's not to love? Here the most esteemed of these oysters are cultivated by the Kelly family on Inner Galway Bay in water that passes all tests for quality. They are sold as Kelly Galway oysters— firmly textured with flinty and metallic overtones but smooth tasting, they are often described as big with soy-sauce tonalities.

10. Japan, Jersey Island, Brazil, Loch Ryan oysters from Scotland, more varieties from North America, even some

from Africa—where is number 10? I am tempted by France, ha-ha, but how about New Zealand? Talk about unpolluted and oxygenated waters. I have been fortunate to travel there for business on numerous occasions, and I am always content with a plate of *Bluff oysters* from the southernmost part of New Zealand, Bluff. Next stop the South Pole. Native to New Zealand and Chile, these oysters (*Tiostrea chilensis*, also known as *ostra chilena*) are harvested by dredging. They can grow quite large and taste of the fresh sea, from which they are harvested from a few meters deep to more commonly twenty or thirty meters. And, of course, the wines in New Zealand are divine. An exotic-fruit sauvignon blanc from Marlborough with Bluff oysters perhaps becomes oysters with wine instead of wine with oysters.

Caveat Emptor

What does an oyster taste like? That's a hard question to answer. Above and earlier, I have tried to use common descriptors for some oysters, and have tried to give brief suggestions of what to expect from certain types and species of oysters.

However, for two reasons, I don't quite trust mine or anyone's shorthand descriptions. The first I have hit upon repeatedly: a particular type or species of oyster can taste quite a bit different depending upon its age, size, and where it grew up.

The water it lived in and on, the minerals and phytoplankton it ingested, the temperature of its home, the season it is tasted, the salinity, et cetera, et cetera, all can change the taste dynamics from one oyster to another a dozen feet away, not to mention a half world apart.

The other reason is: I find that how I eat an oyster can have a dramatic difference in what I taste. If I bring an oyster up to my lips and let it slide out of its shell and into my mouth, or push it out of the shell with an oyster fork into my mouth, then chew, chew, and swallow it down my throat with its salty liquor, that's one taste. If I lift it out of the shell with an oyster fork, let the liquor roll off, put it in my mouth, and chew, then swallow, another experience. Then I drink the liquor. With and without the salty water, liquor, two different experiences.

Certainly I taste the sea powerfully when I drink the liquid with the flesh of the oyster. The salt is long on the finish, powerful, and can taste of iodine. Whatever the mineral characteristics of the water, I taste. The salt in particular, if strong, certainly can mask some of the flesh flavors, or at least add different dimensions to them. I find that the oysters out of the liquor generally taste sweeter, and I can pick up more flavor overtones, such as melony, grassy, or nutty flavors. The finish is not as metallic or strong till I drink the liquor. Two descriptions for the same or similar oysters. Hmm. Both seductively pleasant.

So, the tasting notes are accurate only generally. A Kumamoto is sweeter, smaller, and less metallic than a Belon, that's for sure. Thus there is no substitute for tasting *and* tasting oysters to form your own opinions and perhaps descriptors. Wine tasting is much easier.

LIBATIONS

I prefer wine with oysters, preferably Champagne, *merci beaucoup*. Yet much of the world prefers beer. Okay. So oysters grow in six continents (and beyond), in countless bays and lagoons, and include four hundred species. Today we live in a world of microbreweries using different waters and hops to make countless types and styles, and of course large commercial breweries shipping the world over. Oysters and beer. If you fancy beer with oysters as a match, good luck; you have a lifetime or two of work and pleasure ahead in finding your winning combinations.

Spirits are another historic and pleasurable marriage partner with oysters. Brandy works. And the flavor variations among brandies and barrels and aging are legend. Ditto Scotch whisky. There are many who believe the smoky essence of many Scotches, especially single malts, marry exceptionally well with various oysters. It's a classic: one plus one equals more than more when it comes to taste and experience of food and drink. But as any Scotch connoisseur (not me) knows, the Scotch palette is extensive . . . and so are the subtleties of oysters.

Lots of combinations work well, but again, there is much work and pleasure for those inclined to experiment.

Let's consider wine. It, too, can be as complicated as you want to make it, but there are so many winning combinations of wines from around the world with oysters from around the world, why bother? Just enjoy.

The parameters are pretty simple. Generally, dry white wines work best, whether still or sparkling. Some of the more aromatic wines are attractive but less universal.

The French are the biggest consumers of both French wines and French oysters, but they produce enough to ship them all over the world. The French wines I pointed out earlier—Champagne, Chablis, Sancerre, muscadet, Pouilly-Fuissé, and Entre-Deux-Mers—are safe bets and are likely available in some combination if wines are sold where oysters are sold.

But why not think grape or think local? Or both? America's Pacific Northwest is rich in oysters and oyster wines; for example, pinot gris, riesling (dry), even chenin blanc and sémillon from Washington State. Pinot grigio from Italy, another simple, crisp white, works. Pinot blanc, sure. Or a Spanish albariño, why not? An Austrian grüner veltliner, perhaps. Chardonnays work brilliantly so long as they have crisp acidity and are not too fat and buttery, so be careful of hot-climate chardonnays or overly oaked ones.

The grape of first consideration no matter where it is made—from New Zealand to Chile to the Loire Valley—is sauvignon blanc, which, when well made, has a tart acidity that cuts well the fatty taste of oysters, and so long as the wines aren't too grassy, but more fruity, balance the taste of most oysters. The big metallic oysters, though, like Belons, can be a challenge for any wine. Then I have an answer I have given thousands of times in my life.

When in doubt, drink Champagne. Okay, a well-made sparkling wine from around the world should also stand up to any oyster and enrich the gustatory experience.

12

RECIPES

A friend asked me for a few cooked-oyster recipes. It seems her husband from the American heartland had never tasted an oyster, and he just could not belly up to the bar for a raw one. Her idea was to offer a cooked one, partly disguised with other ingredients, for an introduction. Her plan is a well-tested one. "The recipes worked, and proved the perfect entry and entrée for my little project," she wrote. "Phase two will be raw, of course, but for him, baby steps first."

Most oyster lovers prefer to eat their oysters alive—or raw—served cold on a bed of ice and/or seaweed. There is greatness, too, in a cooked oyster, as many a great chef has proved. We have gone many times to Maison Bru in Provence, and I don't think I have ever been there with my husband when he has not ordered the king crab with spinach, a Marennes oyster, and potato mousse with truffles. Decadence. Whenever I see oysters in any variation of aspic, I vote yes.

The following recipes provide cooked versions of oysters for variety or perhaps for "baby steps." The roasted version is the simplest, but if you are not quite ready for that, try some of the following recipes, where cheese, cream, herbs, butter, spices, or veggies may, with luck, lead the less adventurous to try the next step of eating a simple or raw oyster to experience the true taste of the sea. I cook with only fresh oysters that I shuck, but you can get freshly shucked oysters without shells at some fishmongers, and I have had good reports from people who cook with oysters packed in a jar. Make sure when you cook oysters that the cooking time is short so you don't toughen the tender bivalves.

And oh, oyster stuffing for a turkey? Umm. Right… cooked oysters.

Roasted Oysters

SERVES 4

Again, if you are not ready to taste raw oysters, probably the quickest and easiest way is to try a roasted one. My Parisian friend Amélie always prepares some when she has her international gatherings. She orders a few bourriches of oysters from the brasserie down the street, then serves half raw to her oyster-lover friends and the rest roasted, which everyone seems to enjoy. She has a high rate of success in winning over "neophytes," who are quick to go "raw" the next time.

Rock salt
24 oysters, scrubbed
Salt and freshly ground pepper
Juice of 1 lemon

. . . .

Preheat the oven to 450°F.

Spread a layer of rock salt on a baking sheet and nestle the oysters in it, curved shell down. Place in the oven and bake until the shells just begin to open, 9–10 minutes. Remove the pan from the oven. To open the oysters, hold a roasted oyster with an oven mitt or kitchen towel, insert an oyster knife into the hinge between the shells, and twist the blade to open. Serve immediately on the deep halves of the shells, seasoned to taste with salt, pepper, and fresh lemon juice.

OYSTERS WITH PARMESAN

SERVES 4

Our Roman friends claim that even the French oysters they get in Rome don't taste quite the same as in Paris. More often than not, they prepare a cooked version, and the touch of Parmesan is a nice way to introduce people to the bivalves, though it requires shucked oysters or someone to do the job (husband Maurizio does it in his sleep!), and then a few minutes to prepare a lovely appetizer or meal. Try them with a simple dry white Italian wine or even a premium prosecco, not a bad combination. When I am traveling and see oysters on the menu but am not sure how fresh they are, I order them cooked, as there is usually a variation of this recipe with a local cheese.

Rock salt
24 oysters on the half shell
½ cup dry white wine
2 tablespoons unsalted butter
1 tablespoon minced fresh parsley
¾ cup freshly grated Parmesan

    ·   ·   ·   ·

Preheat the broiler.

Spread a layer of rock salt on a baking sheet and nestle the oyster shells in it. Pour a small spoonful of wine over each oyster and top with a thin slice of butter and a sprinkle of parsley. Cover each with Parmesan and broil in the oven until the cheese melts and becomes golden and the edges of the oysters begin to curl, 3–5 minutes.

OYSTERS WITH CITRUS SAUCE

SERVES 4

Here's another simple way to "spice oysters up," not so different from adding a squirt of fresh lemon juice or some vinaigrette to raw ones. Citrus juices bring out or add another dimension to the taste of oysters, not unlike some accompaniments served in restaurants both in France and in the United States. The juices open up your appetite.

24 oysters on the half shell
3 tablespoons unsalted butter, chilled and cut into small cubes
Juice and zest of 1 lemon
Juice of 1 orange
Pinch of paprika
Salt to taste
Fresh minced parsley for garnish

■   ■   ■   ■

Strain the oyster liquor. Place the oysters with their liquor in a saucepan over medium heat, bring to a gentle simmer, and poach for approximately 2 minutes, or until the oysters' edges just begin to curl, skimming the surface as needed. Meanwhile, clean the oyster shells and arrange on a serving tray. Remove the oysters from the saucepan and place them in a small bowl and keep warm.

Add the butter, lemon juice and zest, orange juice, and paprika to the saucepan containing the oyster liquor. Bring to a simmer over medium-high heat, whisking until the butter melts. Continue to simmer until the sauce thickens slightly, about 5 minutes. Season to taste with salt, add the poached oysters, and stir just to warm. Spoon 1 oyster and some sauce into each shell and serve immediately, garnished with fresh parsley.

Oyster Soup with Crème Fraîche

SERVES 4

Now, as my mother would say, "un délice aux huîtres pour ceux qui aiment la crème" (an oyster delight for cream lovers). Count me in on that one any day, especially on a cold winter night with a slice of good seven-grain bread, a heavy spread of salted butter, and maybe a glass of the same wine used in the preparation. That's a royal dinner. Add a piece of fruit for dessert to complete the meal nutritionally.

24 shucked oysters and their liquor

1 cup dry white wine

¼ cup crème fraîche

4 tablespoons unsalted butter, chilled and cut into small cubes

Salt and freshly ground pepper

1 tablespoon finely chopped fresh chives

■ ■ ■ ■

Strain the oyster liquor. Place the shucked oysters and strained liquor in a saucepan, add the wine, and bring to a boil over medium-high heat for 1 minute, skimming the surface as needed. Remove the saucepan from the heat, add the crème fraîche, and stir to combine. Return the pan to the stove and, over low heat, add the butter, stirring until smooth. Season to taste with salt and pepper and divide among 4 small bowls. Garnish with fresh chives and serve immediately.

OYSTER VICHYSSOISE

SERVES 4

This will appeal to lovers of leeks, cream, and oysters. Count me in on that one, too. Served with a chilled muscadet, this dish makes for a perfect brunch course.

¾ cup crème fraîche, divided
2 tablespoons unsalted butter
3 medium Yukon Gold potatoes, peeled and cut into small cubes
4 leeks, white parts only, cleaned and minced
3–4 cups chicken stock
¼ cup dry white wine
1 tablespoon lemon juice
Salt and freshly ground pepper
16 shucked oysters and their liquor, divided

■　　■　　■　　■

Whip ¼ cup of the crème fraîche and reserve in the refrigerator.

Melt the butter in a saucepan over medium heat, add the potatoes and leeks, and sauté, stirring, for 3 minutes. Add 3 cups of chicken stock, the remaining ½ cup crème fraîche, the wine, and the lemon juice. Season to taste with salt and pepper, increase heat to medium high, and bring to a boil. Reduce heat to medium low and gently simmer until the potatoes are very tender, 25–30 minutes. Carefully transfer the mixture to a blender and purée or pass through a vegetable mill, adding more chicken stock if too thick. Place the pureed soup in a clean saucepan and add the oyster liquor; stir over medium heat until hot. Season to taste.

Place the raw oysters in warm soup dishes and pour the soup on top. The hot soup will "cook" the oysters slightly. Garnish with whipped crème fraîche and serve immediately.

OYSTER OMELET WITH SHIITAKE MUSHROOMS

SERVES 2

This is definitely a great, simple, and warm introduction to the oyster naysayer. I've turned lots of friends into addictive raw oyster lovers with this recipe in New York and Paris. The pancetta and mushrooms may seem to hide the pearls, but chewing them within the egg combination leads to a "Hmm, those little chunks from the sea in there bring an additional flavor." And curious eaters will keep exploring till they reach the "raw" stage. Didn't I say somewhere that life is lived in stages?

⅓ cup diced pancetta (or bacon)
1 tablespoon minced shallot
2 tablespoons unsalted butter, divided

1¼ cups thinly sliced shiitake mushrooms
12 shucked oysters, with 2 tablespoons oyster liquor
6 large eggs
Salt and freshly ground paper
1 tablespoon minced parsley

■   ■   ■   ■

Place the pancetta (or bacon) in a large nonstick skillet and cook over medium heat until golden and crisp, 2–3 minutes. Add the shallot and sauté until fragrant and softened, about 2 minutes. Place the pancetta-shallot mixture in a small bowl and keep warm. Add 1 tablespoon of the butter to the same pan, and, when melted, add the shiitake mushrooms and cook, stirring, for about 3 minutes. Add the oysters and sauté until they are plump and their edges have just started to curl. Remove the mixture from the pan, drain any excess liquid, place in a bowl, and reserve.

In a medium bowl whisk the eggs together with the oyster liquor and season to taste. Add the remaining 1 tablespoon butter to the pan and melt over medium-high heat. Pour the eggs into the pan and cook, lifting the edges with a spatula to allow the uncooked egg to seep underneath, until the bottom of the omelet is golden and the top is just starting to set. Scatter the pancetta-shallot and shiitake-oyster mixtures over the top and carefully slide the omelet onto a large plate, folding one edge over the filling. Sprinkle with parsley and serve immediately.

OYSTERS ROCKEFELLER

SERVES 4

Gabrielle, my dear and gourmande champenoise friend, makes a version of this dish in which she replaces the Pernod with Champagne to have the trio of her favorite foods, oysters, spinach, and Champagne, all in one dish. I like hers a lot, but I still prefer to use an anise-flavored liqueur in this dish.

My first experience with this classic dish was actually not in France, but at Antoine's Restaurant in New Orleans. Little did I know I was eating at the source! The place is a monument. I doubt there is another family-run restaurant in this country today (considering the short life of most restaurants) that opened in 1840 and is still alive and well.

No other American dish has received as many accolades, been so widely imitated and adapted, or evolved as much as this one. Basically, though, it is oysters on the half shell topped with a green sauce with breadcrumbs and then baked.

The dish was created by Antoine's son, Jules Alciatore, in 1899, based on a snail recipe; a shortage of snails gave him the idea to use oysters. Thus parsley seems to have been the original green ingredient, though some claim it was watercress. We'll never know, as Antoine's recipe is still a secret and has no doubt evolved, too. The dish was named after John D. Rockefeller, the richest American at the time, for the richness of the sauce. It seems that a customer gave Jules the idea, exclaiming after eating the dish, "This is as rich as Rockefeller." It is said that the original dish had about eighteen ingredients. This recipe follows my philosophy of "less is more"… not only in the number, but particularly in the amounts (oh, the amount of butter in the original… but if you have ever eaten classic escargots with butter and garlic the old-fashioned way, you know what I am trying to convey).

4 cups fresh baby spinach, washed and steamed until just wilted
⅓ cup chopped shallots
⅓ cup chopped parsley
⅓ cup finely ground fresh breadcrumbs
1 teaspoon Worcestershire sauce
1 tablespoon Pernod
2–3 dashes Tabasco sauce
5 tablespoons unsalted butter, softened
⅔ teaspoon kosher salt
Rock salt
24 oysters on the half shell
1 lemon, cut into wedges

Preheat the oven to 450°F.

Squeeze any excess water from the steamed spinach before placing it in a food processor. Add the shallots, parsley, breadcrumbs, Worcestershire sauce, Pernod, Tabasco sauce, butter, and kosher salt; purée until smooth.

Spread a layer of rock salt on a baking sheet and nestle the oyster shells in it. Top each oyster with 1 teaspoon of purée, place the baking sheet in the oven, and bake until golden, 12–15 minutes. Remove from the oven, transfer the oysters to a platter or individual plates garnished with lemon wedges, and serve immediately.

Oysters à la Normande

SERVES 4

Normandy is the land of apples and cream and the apple-based digestif Calvados. Every region that produces oysters has recipes typical of the local taste and ingredients. I first had this dish (made with the luscious Utah Beach oysters) early in my marriage, while visiting Honfleur and sitting for lunch at a small bistro overlooking the water on a chilly late spring day. It was the perfect dish to warm me up and salute the first rays of spring sun. Beurre d'Isigny is the local butter there, and the taste of the oysters and the bread and butter is still vivid in my memories of that meal.

4 tablespoons unsalted butter
2 Granny Smith apples, peeled, cored, and finely diced

2 tablespoons Calvados
Rock salt
24 oysters on the half shell
½ cup crème fraîche
Salt and freshly ground pepper
Fresh dill for garnish

* * * *

Preheat the broiler.

Melt the butter in a skillet over medium-low heat. Add the diced apples and cook, stirring occasionally, until softened and lightly golden, 7–10 minutes. Add the Calvados and simmer until reduced, 2–3 additional minutes. Remove from the heat and reserve.

Spread a layer of rock salt on a baking sheet and nestle the shucked oysters in it. Top each with ½–1 teaspoon of crème fraîche and ½–1 teaspoon apples, depending on the size of the oyster. Season to taste with salt and pepper and place the baking sheet in the oven. Cook until the oysters are plump and edges have just started to curl and the tops are golden, 3–5 minutes. Remove from the oven, transfer the oysters to a tray, garnish with dill, and serve immediately.

OYSTER BROCHETTES

SERVES 4

Only since the twentieth century have oysters mostly been consumed cold, unless at the seaside, so this brochette recipe is, after a fashion, a return to past traditions.

16 shucked oysters, drained
8 thin slices of bacon, cut in half crosswise
Freshly ground pepper
2 tablespoons minced parsley
1 lemon, cut into wedges

■   ■   ■   ■

Preheat the broiler.

Place the bacon in a skillet over medium-high heat and par-cook just until the edges have started to curl but the slices are still flexible. Remove from the pan and reserve.

After patting the oysters dry with paper towels, wrap 1 piece of bacon around each oyster and secure with a small toothpick. Season with freshly ground pepper and place each oyster on a baking sheet, toothpick side down. Place the baking sheet in the oven and broil for 4–5 minutes. Turn the oysters over and cook for an additional 1 to 2 minutes, until the bacon is crisp and the oysters' edges have just started to curl. Remove from the oven, transfer to a tray, and garnish the oysters with parsley and lemon wedges. Serve immediately.

SHRIMP WITH OYSTERS AND SEAWEED

SERVES 4

This is my humble reproduction of an oyster dish I tasted on one of my first visits to Tokyo, not knowing at the time that oysters were yet another cultural and gastronomic parallel between Japan and France.

   4 ounces fresh, shucked oysters (about 6–8 small- to
      medium-sized oysters) and their liquor
   4 tablespoons chopped parsley
   ⅓ cup plus 2 tablespoons grape-seed oil
   Fresh lemon juice to taste
   Salt and freshly ground pepper
   3 tablespoons unsalted butter, divided
   ½ cup panko breadcrumbs
   8 medium shrimp, shelled and deveined
   1 piece dried seaweed, finely ground in a spice grinder

   .   .   .   .

Strain the oyster liquor and set aside. Place the oysters and parsley in a blender and purée, adding ⅓ cup of grape-seed oil slowly to form an emulsion. Adjust the consistency with the oyster liquor and season to taste with lemon juice, salt, and pepper. Cover and refrigerate until ready to serve.

Melt 2 tablespoons of the butter in a skillet over medium heat. Add the panko breadcrumbs and cook, stirring frequently, until golden and nicely toasted. Season to taste with salt and pepper and reserve on a paper towel-lined plate.

In the same skillet warm the remaining 2 tablespoons of grape-seed oil over medium-high heat and add the shrimp, cooking until golden, about 2 minutes. Turn the shrimp over, add the remaining 1 tablespoon butter, and cook for 10-12 seconds; this side of the shrimp should still be cool while the other should be crisp. Remove the pan from the heat. Spoon the oyster-parsley sauce onto each plate and top with 2 shrimp. Garnish with seaweed and the bread-crumb mixture and serve immediately.

Oysters à la Charentaise

SERVES 4

This dish, which includes mushrooms, shallots, and dry white wine, along with the local butter (beurre des Charentes, another great type of butter), is typically found in many local oyster establishments in the Charente area.

24 shucked oysters and their liquor
Rock salt
4 tablespoons unsalted butter
3 tablespoons minced shallot
2 cups cleaned and minced white mushrooms
2 tablespoons minced parsley
1 tablespoon flour
⅓ cup dry white wine
Salt and freshly ground pepper

■   ■   ■   ■

Preheat the broiler.

Strain the oyster liquor (approximately ½ cup) and add to a saucepan; warm over medium heat. Add the oysters and poach for 1–2 minutes, skimming the surface as needed. Meanwhile, spread a layer of rock salt on a baking sheet and nestle the oyster shells in it. Place an oyster in each shell; pour the oyster liquor into a small bowl and reserve.

Add the butter to the same saucepan and melt over medium heat. Add the shallot and cook until translucent, 4–5 minutes. Add the mushrooms and parsley and sauté for 2–3 minutes. Add flour to the oyster liquor and whisk until smooth. Add the flour-liquor mixture to the mushrooms and stir until combined. Add the white wine, increase the heat to medium high, and bring to a simmer; cook until slightly thickened, 2–3 minutes. Season to taste with salt and pepper, spoon sauce over each oyster, and place the baking sheet in the oven. Broil until hot and bubbling, about 1 minute.

Remove from the oven, transfer to a tray, and serve immediately.

Skillet-Fried Oysters

SERVES 4

24 shucked oysters, drained
2 medium eggs
2 tablespoons 2% milk
Salt and freshly ground pepper
1 cup flour
1 cup cornmeal
Vegetable oil for frying
Lemon wedges
Hot sauce or cocktail sauce

Pat the oysters dry with paper towels and set aside. Break the eggs into a bowl, add the milk, season with salt and pepper, and whisk to combine. Place the flour and cornmeal in two separate shallow bowls (pie dishes also work well) and season both with salt and pepper.

Pour vegetable oil into a skillet to a depth of about 1 inch and heat over medium-high heat until the oil registers 375°F. Dredge one oyster in flour and shake off the excess. Dip into the egg, remove with a fork, and roll in the cornmeal until evenly coated. Shake off any excess and set on a plate. Repeat with the remaining oysters.

Carefully add the oysters in batches and cook until crisp and golden, about 2 minutes per side, depending on the size of the oysters. Be sure to monitor the temperature of the oil: If the oysters brown too fast, reduce the heat; and if they cook too slowly, increase the heat. Remove the oysters from skillet and place on a paper towel–lined plate to drain. Season with salt and serve hot with lemon wedges, hot sauce, or cocktail sauce.

Oven-"Fried" Oysters

SERVES 4

A simple recipe, but the key to superior fried oysters is to find a plump variety and fry them (in a good neutral oil for deep-frying like canola) till crunchy on the outside and silky in the center (like the soft center of a perfect omelet or soufflé).

24 shucked oysters, drained
Extra-virgin olive oil
Salt and freshly ground pepper
1 lemon, cut into wedges

Preheat the oven to 400°F.

Pat the oysters dry with paper towels. Brush a baking sheet with olive oil and arrange the oysters in a single layer on the sheet. Generously brush oysters with olive oil, season with salt and pepper to taste, and cook until nicely browned, about 10 minutes for small to medium oysters and 12 minutes for medium to large oysters. Remove from the oven, transfer the oysters to a tray, and serve immediately with lemon wedges.

OYSTERS WITH CHAMPAGNE
SERVES 4

This is a nostalgic dish for me and possibly my favorite "cooked oyster" recipe, though probably a pale duplication compared to the one I first tasted on one of my early visits to Les Crayères restaurant in Reims.

24 oysters on the half shell, with liquor
Rock salt
½ cup brut Champagne
2 tablespoons minced shallot

1 stick (4 ounces) unsalted butter, chilled and cut into
   small cubes
Salt and freshly ground pepper (optional)

* * * *

Preheat the oven to 450°F.

Remove the oysters from their shells and place in a nonstick saucepan. Strain the oyster liquor and add to the saucepan. Spread a layer of rock salt on a baking sheet. Clean the shells, arrange on the salt-covered baking sheet, and set aside. Add the Champagne to the saucepan and bring to a gentle boil over medium-high heat; cook for 2 minutes, skimming the surface as needed. Remove the saucepan from the heat and place an oyster in each shell. Return the saucepan to the heat, add the shallot, and simmer over medium heat until the liquid has reduced to 4 tablespoons.

Strain the sauce into a clean saucepan and, over medium-low heat, add the butter, a few cubes at a time, whisking constantly, until all the butter has been incorporated and the sauce is emulsified.

Spoon sauce over each oyster and place the baking sheet in the oven to warm the oysters, 1–2 minutes. Remove from the oven, transfer the oysters to a tray, and serve immediately.

OYSTERS WITH CURRY SAUCE

SERVES 4

If you want to transport your taste buds to Southeast Asia, add a little curry, an amazing spice that's good for your health.

Rock salt
24 oysters on the half shell
½ tablespoon unsalted butter
3 tablespoons minced shallot
2 large cloves garlic, minced
¼ cup crème fraîche
Pinch of paprika
1 tablespoon curry
Juice of half a lemon (approximately 1 tablespoon)

＊   ＊   ＊   ＊

Preheat the broiler.

Spread a layer of rock salt on a baking sheet. Remove the oysters from their shells and strain the liquor through a sieve into a small bowl. Clean the shells, arrange on the salt-covered baking sheet, and place an oyster in each shell.

Melt the butter in a saucepan over medium heat. Add the strained oyster liquor, shallot, and garlic and simmer until the liquid is reduced by half. Add the crème fraîche, paprika, curry, and lemon juice, whisking until smooth. Reduce the heat to medium low and simmer until slightly thickened, 2–3 minutes. Spoon sauce over each oyster and place the baking sheet under the broiler until bubbling and the edges of the oysters have just started to curl, 3–5 minutes. Remove from the oven, transfer the oysters to a tray, and serve immediately.

13

CODA À LA FRANÇAISE

Once in a while, a pas de deux. It is a Sunday morning in early fall when the air is crisp but Paris is gray, and Edward and I are walking up our street to the Luxembourg Gardens. It is our most common walk. Today we will pass through the Gardens, then head to a rendezvous on rue Vavin, still in the sixth arrondissement, but a fifteen-minute walk. We pass a stylish middle-aged couple—if forty still passes as middle-aged in our aging world—and hear a snippet of their conversation. "Let's go to Régis for lunch." It strikes me as a perfectly normal neighborhood exchange among Parisians. In that neighborhood if they had said Marco Polo, the Italian restaurant destination for Parisians rather than tourists, I would have also smiled inwardly. The remark also made me think about whether we should go to Régis for lunch.

Régis, meanwhile, was no doubt up and putting in or taking out of the oven one of his trays of apple tarts. He'd be at home somewhere on the outskirts of Paris, perhaps a little bleary-eyed after a Saturday night when he tends to stay open a little later and consume a glass or two or three with friends. No matter, in a couple of hours the entire world knows where he will be: 3 rue Montfaucon in the sixth arrondissement. And on a Sunday, he will probably arrive a bit past the opening, and the regulars—probably half of the people on a Sunday—will be awaiting his entrance and that of the *tarte aux pommes*.

Alain, the oyster shucker, would already be there. Where he lives and what he does outside of standing behind the bar at Régis is something of a mystery. It is just a French thing not to get into a personal conversation with the staff in shops and restaurants or almost anywhere. Even with someone like Régis, who, when he warms up, is funny, talkative, a great storyteller, and plays maître d', the conversations are rarely directly personal, even among the most regular of regulars. When one learns something about Régis it is always gained obliquely. And of course the waitress-du-jour will be there, though she will be so busy it is not possible or appropriate to have a conversation with her beyond "*trois fines de claires* no. 2." It was literally years after one of the waitresses, who was a regular for years, left that I found out she is the previously mentioned daughter of Régis's good friend Christiane.

So, the picture and performance on that Sunday are seemingly perpetual. Sunday in Paris in Saint-Germain-des-Prés.

TAKE TWO: It is a late November morning, and the sky is an unusually beautiful blue. I am walking back from the Boulevard Raspail market and take the relatively quiet rue Servandoni and come across a not-so-unusual French scene. An attractive and youngish-looking woman, probably in her early thirties, is running down the street toward me. Not quite to me, but to the man walking just ahead of me. In a free and typically Parisian fashion, she gives the man a seductive look and smile and a big kiss on each cheek and says, "I have decided we'll have lunch at Régis." "Super, ma biche," the man says, using the French word for a female deer commonly used as an endearment.

Then he pulls her closer to him and initiates the longest French kiss I've ever seen in the streets of Paris, and I have seen people kissing on Parisian streets my entire adult life. Clearly they were *éperdument amoureux* (madly in love), even before heading to eat the aphrodisiac oysters. If the oysters are not an aphrodisiac, they certainly are an extremely nutritious food, and it appeared this couple would need some oysters to keep up their health and energy. The encounter also reminded me of how food and love are often integrated in a Frenchwoman's life. This woman certainly did not give a hoot about people looking at her or what they thought. She was living in the moment.

Huîtrerie Régis lives on in a steady present tense. The oysters are the same. Will there be Belons today? The wines are the same, though mysteriously the vintages change. Will the apple tart arrive? It always does. Huîtrerie Régis is not about becoming but about being.

In one of the most famous of lines in the movie *Casablanca*, Rick (Humphrey Bogart) says to Ilsa (Ingrid Bergman): "We'll always have Paris." Well, Huîtrerie Régis is Paris. Past, present, and future. It is comforting to know it exists in the moment. When I am in New York or in a far-off location, I know I can mentally slip into a seat at Régis and feel deeply, emotionally there. The culture, the people, the traditions, the oysters. Oh, the oysters! I can eat them like Hemingway and Proust. I think I'll take a dozen *spéciales de claires* no. 3.

Délicieuses.

INDEX

Index

ABOUT THE AUTHOR

MIREILLE GUILIANO is the author most recently of the internationally bestselling *French Women Don't Get Facelifts* and of the classic *French Women Don't Get Fat: The Secret of Eating for Pleasure,* the #1 *New York Times* bestseller, which has been translated into thirty-seven languages. A former chief executive at LVMH (Clicquot, Inc.), Guiliano is "the high priestess of French lady wisdom" (*USA Today*) and "ambassador of France and its art of living" (*Le Figaro*). She has appeared on *The Today Show,* CBS's *The Early Show,* NBC's *Dateline,* and CNN, among many national and international broadcasts, and has been profiled in the *New York Times, USA Today, TIME,* and dozens of other publications. She is also the author of *French Women for All Seasons, Women, Work & the Art of Savoir Faire,* and *The French Women Don't Get Fat Cookbook.* Born in France, she enjoys oysters in New York City, Paris, and Provence. www.mireilleguiliano.com.